D0605502

Best-Loved Bible Stories

Best-Loved Bible Stories

EDITED BY DAVE AND NETA JACKSON

Chariot Books™
David C. Cook Publishing Co.

Chariot Books™ is an imprint of David C. Cook Publishing Co.
David C. Cook Publishing Co., Elgin, IL 60120
David C. Cook Publishing Co., Weston, Ontario

BEST-LOVED BIBLE STORIES
© 1978, 1979, 1980, 1981, 1989 by David C. Cook Publishing Co.

All rights reserved. Except for brief excerpts for review purposes, no part of this book may be reproduced or used in any form without written permission from the publisher.

Design by Catherine Colten
Calligraphy by Tim Botts

David C. Cook gratefully acknowledges Tyndale House Publishers, Inc., for permission to print the Hook art on pages 67, 69, and 163.

First printing, 1989
Printed in the United States of America
93 92 91 90   3 4 5

Library of Congress Cataloging-in-Publication Data

Best-loved Bible stories.

   Summary: A collection of stories from the Old and New Testament arranged in chronological order.

   1. Bible stories, English.   [1. Bible stories] I. Jackson, Dave.   II. Jackson, Neta.
BS551.2.B472 1989   220.9'505   89-463
ISBN 1-55513-242-1

Table of Contents

Foreword

What a privilege parents and grandparents have to saturate the minds of their little ones with the riches of Scripture! Is there a better way to learn about obedience than to hear what Noah did? Or to learn the consequences of disobedience than with Jonah and Samson? What comfort there is in knowing the Good Shepherd who cares for His lambs, or the Father who welcomes home His wayward son.

I am thankful for a grandmother who brought Bible stories right down to where I lived and made them real to me. Grandma had a big family Bible that I was allowed to look through carefully. The pictures remain in my mind to this day.

"Grandma," I would say, "who is this?"

"That's little Samuel," she said. And then she told me how Hannah had kept her promise to give her son back to God, and how she brought him a new coat every year.

"I might change my mind," I ventured. "I might want to keep him."

"We must never break a promise to God or to anyone else," Grandma told me. "Because Hannah was faithful, Samuel became a great man of God."

I remember a picture of Daniel, standing calmly in the midst of those hungry lions. Why was he there?

"Because he obeyed God, even though he knew it might cost him his life," Grandma said. "Those lions are like people who might laugh at you for being a Christian, or persuade you to cheat so you don't fail a test. You have to be like Daniel and dare to do right. Then God takes care of the lions."

Grandma was right. God has honored my life and taken care of the lions. I can still hear Grandma say, "That's the way God takes care of His children, you know."

Spending time with a child is rewarding to both generations. To have a book of Bible stories to share together makes it doubly so. Memories will come flooding back when older ones see beloved illustrations they remember from childhood. Younger ones will form memories of quiet times and wonderful stories that will never leave them.

Enjoy this unique volume with a child you love. The benefits to both of you will last into eternity.

Arleta Richardson

"Hear, O Israel: The Lord our God, the Lord is one. Love the Lord your God with all your heart and with all your soul and with all your strength. These commandments that I give you today are to be upon your hearts. Impress them on your children. Talk about them when you sit at home and when you walk along the road, when you lie down and when you get up."

Deuteronomy 6:4-7, NIV

Old Testament

The Creation

*I*n the beginning there was no earth, no sky, no sun, no moon, and no people.

There was only God.

It was God who created everything by the power of His word. When He said something, it happened!

He created the heavens and the earth, but at first it was just a dark, swirling mass. So on the first day, He said, "Let there be light," and there was light. God called the light "day," and the darkness "night."

Then God said, "Let the water fall to the ground and be separate from the sky above." And it was the second day.

And God said, "Let the waters on the earth be gathered together into seas, and let dry land rise up. And let the land produce plants and trees and grow vegetables and grass." All this God did on the third day, and He saw that it was good.

On the fourth day, God said, "Let there be stars and a moon in the night sky, and a sun to shine by day. And let there be seasons and years." And God saw that it was good.

And God said, "Let there be fish in the waters and birds in the sky. And let them each have babies to keep their kind going." And God saw that the work He had done on the fifth day was good.

All the animals were created on the sixth day. Then God decided to create humans—beings like Himself who could be masters over all the other creatures—the animals, the fish, and the birds. So God made both the man and the woman in His own image. And He blessed them and told them to have children so there would be people in all the world. He told them to take care of all God's creatures. And He gave them fruits and vegetables and grains for their food.

God saw all that He had made, and it was excellent.

And so on the seventh day, God rested from all His work. And He blessed the seventh day and made it holy because on it He rested from all His work.

Story based on Genesis 1—2:3.

❦

Pray: Thank You, God, for making such a beautiful world with so many different animals and such interesting people. Help me to take care of Your world and love other people.

Illustration by Fred Schnaple, 1937

10

Adam and Eve Disobey God

The man God created was called Adam. And God brought all the animals and birds to the man and let him name them.

The woman God created was Eve. God knew that it was not good for people to be alone. So it was His plan from this time on for a man and a woman to leave the homes of their parents and get married, love each other, and have children.

Adam and Eve lived in Eden, the most beautiful garden in all the world. God made it for them. He gave them only one rule. They were not to eat the fruit from one certain tree in the garden.

One day as Eve was walking alone in the garden, she came to this special tree. In it was a snake. "Has God told you that you may not eat the fruit from this tree?" the snake asked.

"We may eat from every tree but this one," Eve said. "If we eat from this one, God said we would die."

"You won't die," the snake said. "If you eat the fruit, you will be wise."

Eve looked at the fruit. It looked so good. She tasted it. "I must give some to Adam," she said. She did, and Adam ate it, too.

Suddenly Adam and Eve were afraid. They ran and hid.

But God called them. "Have you eaten this fruit? I told you not to eat it," God said.

"Eve gave it to me," Adam said, trying to blame her.

"The snake told me to eat it," Eve said, trying to blame someone else.

Then God had to do something He did not want to do. He had to punish them for disobeying Him.

"You must leave the garden I made for you," God said. "You must go out and work hard for your food."

So Adam and Eve left the garden called Eden. They looked back. In the path was a sword of fire! Guards stood by it. Adam and Eve could never go back!

God was sorry for them. "I love you," God said. "If you love and obey Me, I will help you." But God would not *make* them obey. Adam and Eve had to choose for themselves whether they would obey or disobey God.

Story based on Genesis 2 and 3.

❧

Something to Think About: What would the world have been like if Adam and Eve had obeyed God? Think of one thing God wants you to do.

Illustration by Fred Schnaple, 1937

12

Cain and Abel

Adam and Eve were all alone in a strange land. They had to work hard to raise the food they needed.

"If only we had done what God wanted," Eve said. "If only we could walk and talk with Him each day as we did in the garden."

"We can still worship Him and pray to Him," Adam said.

And they did.

After a while Adam and Eve had a son! They named him Cain. When their next son was born, they called him Abel. The boys grew up. They helped their mother and father. Cain liked to raise grain. Abel liked to take care of the sheep.

"All that we have comes from God," Adam and Eve told their sons. "When you worship God, give Him the best that you have."

Abel listened. He loved God and gave Him the best he had. But Cain didn't. God liked what Abel did. But He did not like what Cain did. This made Cain angry. And he was very jealous of his brother, Abel.

"Why are you so angry?" God asked Cain. "If you do what is right, I will be pleased by it. But if you don't do what is right, you will soon find yourself committing a worse sin."

And God was right. One day when Cain was out in the field with Abel, his anger became so strong that he attacked his brother and killed him.

Cain was sure no one had seen him. But he was afraid.

Illustration by Henry Luhrs, 1942

14

Then God said, "Where is your brother?"

"I don't know," Cain lied. "Do I have to take care of him?"

Then Cain thought, "God knows I have killed Abel." Cain was very afraid.

"You have done a terrible thing," God said. "You must go away and never come back."

"Oh, no!" Cain cried. "Anything but that."

"I will see that no harm comes to you," God said. "But you must go."

Adam and Eve cried for the son who was dead. They cried for the son who had done wrong. After a while they had another son. They called him Seth.

"I pray that all his life he obeys God," Adam said.

Adam's prayer was answered. Seth grew up to be a man who loved God.

Story based on Genesis 4:1-16, 25.

❧

Something to Think About: What was Cain's first sin? How did that sin grow? When Cain realized God was unhappy with his disobedience, what should he have done?

Noah and the Ark

After many, many years God became sad. The world He had made was beautiful. But the people He had made did not do what God wanted. They quarreled.

"Why should we work?" they said. "We'll steal what we want from our neighbors."

"The sun makes our crops grow," they said. So they worshiped the sun instead of God who made the sun.

At last there was only one good family left. It was Noah's family. One day God said to Noah, "I must get rid of all that is wicked. I will send a flood to cover the earth. You must make a boat. It will keep you and your wife and your three sons and their wives safe. You and your family will make a new start."

So Noah began to build the ark.

The wicked people laughed at Noah. "Poor Noah thinks he can float a boat on dry land," they said.

But Noah went right on doing what God told him to do. At last the ark was finished. God spoke again to Noah: "Go into the ark. Take seven pairs of animals and birds that are good to eat. Take one pair of each kind that is not good to eat."

Noah did as God told him to do. Then God closed the door of the ark.

It began to rain. It rained for forty days and forty nights until water covered the earth—even the highest mountains. It rained until everything wicked had been washed away. But Noah and his family were safe in the ark.

At last the rain stopped. The water went down. The ark touched ground. Finally, God told Noah that his family and the animals could come out of the ark.

The birds stretched their wings and flew. The animals pushed and ran to reach the brown earth and the new green grass. Noah built an altar. He and his family worshiped God.

God was pleased with Noah. "I will never again send water to cover the earth," God said. Then a wonderful thing happened. A rainbow stretched across the sky. It was red, orange, yellow, green, blue, indigo, and violet.

"When you see the rainbow you will remember My promise," God said.

Noah was happy. "God never breaks His promises," Noah said. And God never has!

Story based on Genesis 6:1—9:17.

❧

Pray: Thank You for giving me second chances to do right. Help me to obey You.

Illustration by Fred Schnaple, 1937

16

Abraham's Call

God wanted a man who was strong and good and brave. He wanted this man to be the leader of a new nation. The man God chose was Abraham.

One night God spoke to Abraham. "Get out of this country. Go to one that I will show you. I will make you the leader of a great nation. I will bless you. And I will make your name great. Everyone on the earth will be blessed through you," God said.

Abraham's heart almost stopped beating. God was calling *him* to start a new nation!

Abraham ran to tell his wife, Sarah.

"But where are we going?" Sarah asked.

"I don't know," Abraham said. "But we're going."

Some people laughed at Abraham. "He is going someplace, but he doesn't even know where," they said to one another.

Abraham didn't mind. His nephew, Lot, didn't mind either. "May I go with you?" Lot asked.

"Of course," said Abraham. He was glad, for he and Sarah had no children. And Lot was like a son to them.

So Abraham and his family, his servants, his camels, his cows, and sheep started out.

"What if we can't find water for our animals?" one servant asked.

Illustration by Fred Schnaple, 1937

"What if wild animals attack us?" another servant asked.

Abraham knew what his servants were saying. But on and on they went, for miles, and miles, and miles. At last they came to a land between a river and the sea. The land was called Canaan.

"This is the land God promised us," Abraham told his people. So he took large stones and piled them up to build an altar, a place where he could worship God and always be reminded of God's goodness to him.

Abraham stood before the altar. "O God," he prayed, "thank You for bringing us to this land. Help me be a good leader."

Abraham was strong and good and brave. And God was pleased with the man He chose.

Story based on Genesis 11:31—12:8.

❦

Pray: Lord, help me to follow Your leading so that I am ready to go where You want me to go.

18

A Bride for Isaac

braham walked around his camp. Mothers and fathers were laughing and talking. Boys and girls were playing. "Everyone is happy. But my son, Isaac, is not happy," Abraham said to himself.

At last Abraham said, "I know what is wrong. Isaac's mother is dead. I am growing old. Isaac has no family of his own. Soon he will be alone. No wonder he is sad."

Abraham called a servant. "Go to the city of my brother, Nahor. Find a wife there for my son, Isaac," Abraham said.

"How will I know if I have found the right woman?" the servant asked.

"God will help you," Abraham said.

So the servant went to the city of Abraham's brother. He stopped near a well to rest. He prayed, "O God, may it be that when I say to a girl, 'Please give me a drink,' the right girl for Isaac will be the one who offers to water my camels, too."

The servant went up to the well. A beautiful young woman was there. She gave him a drink of water. Then she did a very unusual thing; she offered to water his camels, too. It was a big job, and the servant was very impressed.

"Tell me your name," the servant said. "And please see if I may stay at your house."

"My name is Rebekah. I am the granddaughter of Nahor. I live with my brother, Laban. Come, I know

there is room for you at his house."

The servant went to Laban's house. He told Laban, "I am the servant of Abraham, the brother of Nahor. I have come to find a wife for Abraham's son, Isaac. I asked God to help me find the right woman. God has. The woman is Rebekah."

"Will you go with this man?" Laban asked Rebekah.

"Yes," she said.

So the servant took Rebekah back to Abraham's camp. When Isaac saw Rebekah he loved her very much. They were married, and Isaac was happy.

Abraham was happy, too.

Story based on Genesis 24.

❧

Something to Think About: Was God concerned about Isaac's happiness? Do you think He cares if you are happy, too?

Illustration by Elias Sallman, 1945

20

Jacob and Esau

Jacob and Esau were twins. But they did not look alike. And they did not act alike. Esau was strong. He became a mighty hunter.

Jacob's name meant "trickster." He liked to dream. He liked to make believe. He pretended that someday he would be the leader of his people.

But Esau had been born first. And the law said that it was the oldest son's birthright to be the leader of the people.

Jacob knew this, but he kept on scheming. "I *will* be the leader," he said to himself, as he tried to figure out a way he could get the birthright.

Then one day while Jacob was cooking some good-smelling stew, Esau came in from hunting. He was hungry. "Quick, give me something to eat," he said to Jacob.

"Trade me your birthright as the oldest son," Jacob said. "Then I will give you some food."

"Look, I'm starving. You can have my birthright. Only give me something to eat," Esau said without considering what a serious thing he was doing. Esau gave away his important right to be leader of the people. He gave it away for nothing but a dish of stew.

Years went by. One day Isaac called Esau to him. "I am getting old," Isaac said. "Go, get some meat. Cook it and bring it to me. Then I will give you my blessing. It will make you leader someday."

Esau forgot that he gave that right to Jacob. He hurried away. When Esau was gone Jacob cooked some meat. Then he put on Esau's clothes and went to his father.

"Give me the blessing," he said.

Isaac was old. He could hardly see. "Are you really Esau?" he asked.

Jacob lied. He made his voice sound like Esau's. "Yes, I am," he said.

So Isaac gave the blessing to Jacob. When Esau came back, he was angry. "I will kill Jacob for this," he shouted.

To escape his brother's anger, Jacob fled to a far country and lived with his uncle Laban. There Jacob waited, hoping his brother would forget what had happened so it would be safe for him to come home.

Story based on Genesis 25:21-34; 27:1-45.

❧

Something to Think About: What wrong things did both twins do?

Illustration by Fred Schnaple, 1937

Jacob Comes Home

Because Jacob had tricked his brother out of his birthright, his brother was so angry he wanted to kill him.

So he fled to a far land and lived with his uncle, Laban.

Laban had two daughters. The older was Leah. The younger was Rachel, and she was very beautiful. At this time it was not wrong for cousins to marry each other, and soon Jacob fell in love with Rachel.

It was also the custom for a man to pay the family a high price to marry a daughter. So Jacob said to Laban, "I'll work seven years for you in return for Rachel."

"Okay," said Laban.

Seven years was a long time, but Jacob loved Rachel so much that the time seemed to go by quickly.

However, at the wedding Laban gave Jacob his older daughter, Leah, without Jacob knowing it. After the wedding, Jacob said to Laban, "What have you done to me? I served you for Rachel. Why have you tricked me?"

"It's just our custom," said Laban. "The older daughter must always get married first." At this time, some men had more than one wife. So Laban said, "I'll tell you what, you can marry Rachel also if you'll work for me for another seven years."

Poor Jacob the "trickster." Now he had been tricked, too.

But he loved Rachel so much, he agreed.

When Jacob finished his second seven years, he said to Laban, "I'm going to leave now."

But Laban said, "Don't go. God is with you, and under your care my flocks have grown greatly. I'll pay you whatever you want if you'll work for me."

"Okay," said Jacob, "Give me all the spotted or dark sheep and goats, and you keep all the white ones."

"It's a deal," said Laban. But that same day he removed and hid all the spotted and dark animals.

However, Jacob thought of a trick to make sure that the strongest animals had spotted and dark babies, and soon his herds were much larger than Laban's. But this made Laban's sons angry. All the family wealth was going to Jacob.

Then the Lord said to Jacob, "Go back to your father's land and I will be with you."

Jacob had served Laban twenty years when he gathered his wives and family, his flocks and all he had and fled without even telling Laban good-bye.

Story based on Genesis 29—31:21.

❧

Something to Think About: The Lord was with Jacob, so why do you think he had to trick everyone to get what he needed? What did tricking other people do?

Illustration by Fred Schnaple, 1937

24

Joseph Becomes a Slave

Jacob did become an important leader of God's people. And eventually he had twelve sons. Joseph was his favorite and his eleventh son. One day Joseph's brothers were far from home taking care of their father's sheep. But when they talked about home, they became angry.

"Why doesn't Joseph have to work as hard as we do? Why doesn't Father give us beautiful coats like the one he gave Joseph?" they asked. All at once one of the brothers pointed across the field.

"Look!" he cried. "Here comes our brother, Joseph, now. He is probably coming to spy on us."

"Let's get rid him," one of the brothers said. "We will tell Father a wild animal killed him."

So when Joseph reached his brothers they grabbed him and took off his beautiful coat and threw him into a pit.

"Please don't," Joseph cried. "I have not done anything wrong. Father sent me. . . ."

But the brothers wouldn't listen. And when some traders came along, they pulled Joseph out of the pit and sold him to the traders for twenty pieces of silver.

The traders took Joseph to the distant land of Egypt. There, in a big city the traders sold Joseph as a slave. Joseph held his head up. He might be a slave, but he was not a coward.

An officer of the king looked at Joseph. "How strong and straight he is," the officer said. So the officer bought Joseph and took him to his home near the palace.

Joseph worked very hard for his master. He prayed to God to help him be brave and to do his work well. And God did.

One day the officer's wife tried to get Joseph to do something that was wrong.

"No," Joseph said. "I will not cheat my master. And I will not disobey my God."

This made the woman angry. She told her husband a lie about Joseph. She said that Joseph *had* done the wrong thing she had suggested. Joseph's master believed the lie, and he had Joseph put in prison.

The prison was wet and dark. The bright sun never shone through the prison bars. Things looked bad for Joseph.

But Joseph remembered that God was with him. God loved him. God would help him.

Story based on Genesis 37 and 39.

❦

Pray: Dear Lord, help me remember when people are mean to me that You still love me and will help me.

Illustration by Winslow, 1942

26

Joseph Forgives His Brothers

The king of Egypt was called Pharaoh. One day Pharaoh's butler and baker were thrown into the prison with Joseph. They both had dreams, and Joseph told them what their dreams meant.

"You will go back to work for Pharaoh," Joseph told the butler. "And when you do, remember me, and help me get out of here." But as soon as the butler left the prison, he forgot about Joseph.

Two years went by. One night Pharaoh had a dream. No one could tell him what it meant. Then the butler remembered Joseph and told Pharaoh about him.

"Bring Joseph to me," Pharaoh said.

Joseph told Pharaoh the meaning of his dream. Pharaoh was pleased and he said, "God is with you, so I will make you second only to me in all the land."

So Joseph became a ruler in the land where he had once been a slave. But, of course, Joseph's brothers did not know about this.

Then one day there was a great famine, and Joseph's brothers traveled to Egypt to buy food. They brought their youngest brother, Benjamin, with them. Benjamin was Jacob's twelfth son.

Joseph looked at his brothers. He had to know if they were still mean. So he sold them the grain they wanted. But before they left, he put a silver cup in Benjamin's sack.

When the brothers had gone a little way, Joseph sent a servant to stop them. "My master's cup has been stolen," he said. "And the man who has it will be my master's slave."

The servant found the cup in Benjamin's sack and took him back to Joseph's palace. But the other brothers followed.

"Please, sir," one brother said to Joseph. "Our father, Jacob, is very old. He loves Benjamin very much. Let me take Benjamin's place."

Finally, Joseph knew that his brothers had changed. They were not selfish and cruel. He forgave them. Then he told them, "I am your brother, Joseph."

The brothers feared that Joseph would punish them, but Joseph said, "Do not be afraid. You meant to do evil to me, but our great God used it for good, so that our family could be saved from this great famine. Hurry home, now, and bring our father to Egypt."

So Jacob and his sons and their families lived together happily with Joseph in Egypt.

Story based on Genesis 40—47; 50:15-21.

❧

Something to Think About: God changed the brothers' sin into good, but what would have happened if Joseph wouldn't have forgiven them? Can you think of something good that happened when you forgave someone? What was it?

Illustration by Watrous, 1942

28

Miriam, the Bravest Girl

Joseph saved his father, Jacob, and his eleven brothers and their families from a bad famine in their homeland by bringing them to Egypt where he was an important official in Pharaoh's government. In Egypt, Jacob's descendants were called Hebrews. They lived there for many generations and became a great nation, just as God had promised.

But finally a new Pharaoh became king. He did not remember Joseph and how his wise planning had saved everyone from the famine.

This new Pharaoh feared that there were so many Hebrews that they might take over Egypt. So he made slaves of the Hebrews hoping that the hard work would keep them from increasing in numbers.

But the hard work made the Hebrew people stronger and they kept growing in numbers.

Miriam was a little Hebrew girl who lived in Egypt at this time. One day she heard some terrible news. She ran home at once.

"Mother!" she cried. "Pharaoh is going to kill all Hebrew boy babies. What will happen to our baby?"

Miriam's mother held her little boy close. "We'll hide him," she whispered.

One day the mother said to Miriam, "I have a plan to save our baby. You must help me."

"Oh, I will. I will," Miriam cried.

That day the mother took a basket, the baby, and Miriam to the river. She put the baby in the basket and set the basket in the water. "Stay close by and do as I told you," Miriam's mother said.

"I have asked God to help me be brave, and I know He will," Miriam said.

Miriam waited. At last a princess came to the river. She was Pharaoh's daughter. She saw the basket. "Bring it to me," the princess told her maid. When the princess opened the basket, the baby cried.

"It is a Hebrew baby," the maid said.

"There, there, little one," the princess said. "I will take care of you."

Miriam stepped up to the princess. "Shall I get a Hebrew mother to take care of the baby for you?" she asked.

"Please do," the princess said. So Miriam brought her mother, just as her mother had planned.

"Take care of him until he is old enough to live in the palace," the princess said to Miriam's mother. "He will be my son, and I will call him Moses."

"O God," Miriam prayed, "thank You for helping me save my little brother."

Story based on Exodus 1:1—2:10.

❧

Something to Think About: How did Miriam become brave enough to save her little brother? What is one scary thing that God has helped you do?

Illustration by M. Wilhoite, 1946

Moses and the Burning Bush

Moses was raised in Pharaoh's palace. He received the very best schooling and became a fine young man. But even though he was raised as an Egyptian prince, he never forgot that he was a Hebrew. He never forgot that the other Hebrews were slaves in Egypt. Often he would ride out to watch the Hebrew slaves work in the hot sun. He felt he had to do something to help his people.

One day he saw a guard beat one of the Hebrew slaves. Moses was very angry. He thought no one was looking. So Moses killed the guard. He buried him in the sand.

The next day Moses came upon two Hebrews who were fighting. He tried to stop them, but one asked Moses, "Who made you ruler over us? Are you going to kill me, too?"

"Someone saw me kill that Egyptian guard," Moses said to himself. He was afraid. "If Pharaoh finds out, he may try to kill me."

Pharaoh did find out. He told his soldiers to kill Moses. But Moses was afraid and ran away. He ran and ran until he came to another country.

One day Moses sat down by a well to rest. Some young women brought their sheep to the well. Moses helped the women. When their father heard about Moses he asked Moses to come to eat with him. So Moses went to visit the man, a shepherd named Jethro.

Later, Moses married Zipporah, one of Jethro's daughters. And Moses also took care of Jethro's sheep.

One day Moses was watching Jethro's sheep out in the hills. Then he saw a strange thing. A bush was on fire. But it did not burn up. Then a Voice spoke from the bush. "Moses!" The Voice was the Voice of God.

Moses stood very still. "Here I am," he said. Moses did not move.

"I want you to go to Egypt," God said. "I want you to lead the Hebrews out of Egypt. Because I am sending you, I will be with you and help you."

Moses was afraid—but he knew he must obey God.

Story based on Exodus 2:11—4:16.

❧

Something to Think About: What happened when Moses tried to save his people without God's help? Tell about a time when fighting did not solve problems between your friends.

Illustration by Fred Schnaple, 1937

32

Moses and Pharaoh

"You must go to Egypt," God told Moses. "You must lead the Hebrews out of Egypt."

"But I am not a good speaker," protested Moses.

"Who made your mouth?" asked God.

"You did," said Moses.

"Then don't you think I can help you use it to speak with?" asked God.

"O Lord, please send someone else," Moses begged.

"You're My man," said God, getting angry. "But I'll tell you what. I'll give you a helper. Someone to do your speaking for you."

Moses was afraid. But he knew he must do what God said. So Moses told his family what God had said. Then he started for the land of Egypt.

On the way Moses saw a man coming toward him. Then Moses saw who it was. "Aaron!" said Moses. He ran to meet his brother. Aaron ran, too. "Moses!" he shouted. "God sent me here to meet you."

"I know," Moses said. "God wants me to lead the Hebrew people out of Egypt. You must help me."

"It will not be easy," said Aaron. "The Hebrews make good slaves for Pharaoh. He will not want to let us go."

Illustration by Fred Schnaple, 1937

So Moses and Aaron went to see Pharaoh. When they told Pharaoh what they wanted, Pharaoh became very angry. He made the Hebrew people work harder than ever. The Hebrews blamed Moses. "See what you have done to us," they said to him.

Then Moses prayed to God. "Oh, God," he said, "what shall I do?"

"Go back to Pharaoh," God told Moses. "Then do what I tell you to do."

So Moses and Aaron went back to Pharaoh. "If your God is so great," said Pharaoh, "then show me what He can do."

Aaron threw his stick on the ground. It began to crawl. It was a snake. Then Pharaoh told his magicians to do the same thing. When they threw down their rods they turned into snakes, too.

Pharaoh laughed. But Aaron's snake ate up the other snakes. Then Pharaoh could see that God was more powerful than his magicians.

Story based on Exodus 3:10—7:13.

❧

Pray: Dear Lord, help me to obey You and not be afraid of what people will think.

Moses at the Red Sea

Many times Moses went to Pharaoh, saying, "Let my people go." Each time Pharaoh said okay, but then he broke his promise.

It was time for God to do something special. God told Moses to tell the people to kill a lamb for a special feast. Then each family was to put the blood from the lamb on the sides and top of their doors.

"Why are you doing that?" a Hebrew boy asked.

"God is sending the angel of death to Egypt tonight," his father said. "The blood shows the angel where the Hebrews live. The angel will pass over our houses. But he will not pass over the houses of the Egyptians."

The Hebrews packed their food and clothes. They ate their special feast as God told them to do. Then the angel of death came. He passed over the houses of the Hebrew people. But when he came to the houses without the blood on the doors, the oldest boy in every Egyptian home died. Pharaoh was afraid. "Take your people and go," he told Moses.

The Hebrews ran from their houses. "Praise God, we are free!" they shouted. "Thank You, God, for helping us."

God showed Moses which way to go. In the daytime God's cloud went before them. At night the cloud became a bright fire.

The people traveled until they came to the Red Sea. Suddenly a man cried out, "Look! Pharaoh's army is coming after us!" It was true!

"Where can we go?" the people cried. "Mountains are on either side of us, and the sea is in front of us. We're trapped. Why did you bring us here to die?" they yelled at Moses.

"O God," prayed Moses, "tell me what to do."

"Do not be afraid," God said. Then a wonderful thing happened. The cloud moved behind the Hebrews. It was like a big wall between them and Pharaoh's men.

Then God told Moses to hold out his rod over the waters of the sea. When Moses did so the wind began to blow. It blew the waters back until there was a wide, dry path through the sea.

"Now hurry over to the other side," Moses shouted.

The Hebrews ran across. Pharaoh's army tried to follow, but when Moses held out his rod again, the waters came crashing back. Every member of Pharaoh's army drowned.

God's people were safe at last.

Story based on Exodus 7—14.

❧

Something to Think About: Is anything too hard for God? Why do you think God sometimes doesn't do what we ask Him to do if nothing is too hard for Him?

Illustration by Fred Schnaple, 1937

God Provides for His People

*I*t was a happy time for the Hebrews. Children played and waded in the water of the sea. "God is leading us to our new land," said some of the people. "We will build homes. We will never have to work for Pharaoh again."

The Hebrews walked on through a desert where they became very thirsty. At last they came to a pool of water. They drank some of the water. "Ugh," they said. "This water is not good."

Moses prayed to God. Then God told Moses to pull up a little tree and throw it into the pool. "Now, drink the water God has made good for you," Moses told the people.

So the people drank the water. It was very good. So the people were happy again.

But soon their food was gone. "We must have something to eat," they complained. Then God sent many quail for the people to eat. But the people were still worried. "What will we eat when the quail is gone?" they asked.

The next morning they found the ground was white. It was covered with something that looked like frost.

"Manna?" they asked, for *manna* meant "what is it?"

"It is food from God," Moses said. "Take what you need. God will send more."

God did send more. And the people called it manna.

When the people traveled on to a new place there was again no water there for them to drink. But they forgot how the Lord had already provided for them, and they began to quarrel with Moses.

"Why did you bring us up out of Egypt to make us and our children and livestock die of thirst?" they said.

Then Moses cried out to the Lord. "What am I to do with these people?" prayed Moses. "They are almost ready to stone me."

But the Lord told Moses to take some of the other leaders of the people and go on ahead to a rock at Horeb. "There," said the Lord, "you are to strike the rock, and water will come out of it for the people to drink."

So Moses did what the Lord said, and the Lord provided water for the people to drink.

Story based on Exodus 15:22—17:7.

❦

Something to Think About: Why did the people not remember how God had made the bitter water sweet and provided food for them in the desert when they came to a new place and needed water? Do you sometimes forget that God is caring for you?

Illustration by Fred Schnaple, 1937

The Ten Commandments

One day the Hebrew people came to the foot of a great mountain called Sinai.

"This is a wonderful place," said Moses. "I was here when God told me to go to Egypt to rescue you. I am sure God has something to tell us."

So Moses climbed the mountain. There God spoke to Moses.

"In addition to providing the people with food and water, I want to tell them how best to live. If they obey Me," God said, "they shall be My special people."

So Moses went back down and told the people, and they responded by saying, "All that God wants us to do, we will do."

And these were the Ten Commandments for how God wanted His people to live:

1. Do not worship anyone but God.
2. Do not make idols and worship them.
3. Do not use God's name in wrong ways.
4. Rest from your work and worship God on His day.
5. Love and obey your parents.
6. Do not kill people.
7. Husbands and wives must love each other and be faithful.
8. Do not steal.
9. Do not lie.
10. Do not want what other people have.

Illustration by Fred Schnaple, 1937

But Moses was up on the mountain for many days talking to God, and the people became afraid. "Maybe Moses isn't coming back," some of them said. "Let's make an idol we can worship—something we can see like the idols in Egypt."

So they took their gold and melted it and made a golden calf. Then they had a great feast and danced and sang and worshiped the idol. They forgot that it was God who loved them and sent them food when they were hungry.

But God knew what the people were doing. "My people are worshiping a golden calf," He said to Moses.

Moses raced back to the camp, picked up the golden calf, and destroyed it. "You have committed a great sin," he scolded the people, and many of them got sick and died.

The rest were sorry for what they had done. They wanted God to forgive them. So Moses went to a place where he could be alone and talk to God. "O God," he said, "forgive Your people. Be with them and guide them as You have in the past."

"I will be with them," God said. "This is My holy promise."

Story based on Exodus 19—33.

❦

Pray: Please help me to be eager to do all You want me to do. Especially help me remember and obey Your rules for how to live.

40

Spying Out the Promised Land

The Hebrew people were on their way to a wonderful land. They called it the Promised Land because God had promised them it would be their home.

One day Moses, their leader, stopped. "Is this the Promised Land?" the people asked.

"No," Moses said. "But we are close to it. We must send some spies to scout out the land. The people who live there do not like God. They will not like God's people."

So Moses chose twelve brave men. They started out early in the morning. For forty days they walked through the land called Canaan. They saw big cities with walls that were high and wide.

"The men of this land are giants," one of the scouts said.

But the scouts saw trees that were heavy with fruit. They saw vines covered with big bunches of grapes.

"Let us take some of the fruit back with us," one of the scouts said.

They did. And when the Hebrew people saw the fruit they were glad. They could hardly wait to go into the land that was so rich.

"Wait," cried some of the scouts. "The men who live there are giants. They will never let us live in their land."

"Listen!" two scouts cried out. "What these men say is true. But God is with us. He will help us take the land." The names of these faithful spies were Joshua and Caleb.

But the people were afraid. They would not listen. They would not go into the land God had promised them.

Then God spoke to Moses: "My people do not trust Me. So they cannot go into the land I have promised them. For forty years they will wander from place to place in this desert without a home. When this generation dies and their children grow up, then they shall enter the land."

So the Hebrews turned back from the Promised Land and wandered in the wilderness for forty years. During all that time Moses faithfully led the people. God protected them from their enemies and provided manna for them to eat and water to drink.

God performed many miracles to show His power and love for them. One miracle was that He kept their clothes and shoes from wearing out, but they did not get to enter the land because they had doubted God.

Story based on Numbers 13:1—14:34.

❦

Something to Think About: Since God remained with the people while they wandered in the wilderness, do you think He would have helped them defeat the giants in the Promised Land?

Illustration by Turner, 1946

42

The Battle of Jericho

After Moses died, Joshua—one of the faithful spies—became the leader of God's people.

"Today is a special day," Joshua told the people. "Today we cross the Jordan River into the land God promised to us."

"But how will we get across the river?" they asked. "The water is deep and fast."

"Follow the priests carrying God's Holy Ark," said Joshua's officers. The ark was a special box the people carried with them. It showed them that God was near.

So the people followed the priests. And when the priests stepped into the water, a miracle happened, the river stopped flowing.

"Come," said Joshua. "We will all cross over into our new land." So the people marched across the dry riverbed. They marched into their new land.

"God is helping us," the people said.

The city of Jericho was the first city the Hebrew people came to in their new land. Its walls were high and wide. Soldiers marched on top of the walls. The soldiers looked big and strong.

"How can we ever take that city?" some Hebrews asked each other. "How can we ever get over those walls? How can we get past the soldiers?"

Illustration by Loehle, 1968

God spoke to Joshua, the leader of the Hebrews. God knew that Joshua was brave. He knew Joshua did what He told him.

44

"March around Jericho once every day," God said. "March every day for six days. On the seventh day, march seven times." So Joshua had the people do what God said.

Every day for six days the Hebrews marched around Jericho. The soldiers went first. Then seven priests marched with trumpets. Then some priests marched with God's Holy Ark. More soldiers marched after God's Holy Ark.

The soldiers of Jericho looked down from the high walls. At first they laughed. Then they became afraid. "What are those Hebrews doing?" they wondered.

On the seventh day the Hebrews marched around and around the city six times. Then, on the seventh time around, the priests blew on their trumpets. The sound was loud and clear. The men shouted.

All at once something happened. The walls around the city began to shake. Then with a loud crash they fell down, and with God's help, the Hebrews took the first great city in their Promised Land.

After that, God continued to help the Hebrews take the land that He had provided for them.

Story based on Joshua 1, 3, and 6.

❦

Pray: Help me to follow You, dear Lord, and trust that You will help me when problems in my life seem like giants or high walls.

Gideon's Trumpets and Pitchers

As the Hebrew people developed into a nation, they were called the Israelites. And God promised them peace and good crops and everything they needed, provided they would obey and worship Him only. But sometimes the Hebrew people did not obey God. In fact, sometimes they even worshiped the idols of their heathen neighbors. This displeased God very much.

One time when the Israelites began worshiping the idol Baal, God allowed their enemy, the Midianites, to overrun their land as a punishment. For seven years the Midianites occupied the land of Israel and robbed the people of their sheep and cows and grain.

Finally, the people repented of their evil, and God forgave them and decided to save them. During this time there lived a good man named Gideon who was a simple farmer's son.

One day he was threshing grain in a secret place so that the Midianites would not find it and steal it. "When I thresh this grain," thought Gideon, "I must hide it quickly in a cave. What's going to happen to us? O God," he prayed, "please save us."

As Gideon finished threshing his grain, he looked up. Someone was standing nearby. It was an angel of the Lord. "God hasn't forgotten you," said the angel. "He wants to help you. He wants you to lead your people."

Gideon was not sure he should lead his people. Again and again he asked God to show him that he should be the one that would lead them.

At last Gideon was sure. One day he called to his people, "Come," he said. "We will fight the Midianites."

The Israelites came. They came from hills and caves. They came from everywhere. God helped Gideon choose three hundred of the bravest men. The others Gideon sent back home.

Gideon gave each man a trumpet and a pitcher with a torch inside. That night Gideon and his men crept down toward the Midianite camp. "Do as I do," said Gideon.

Suddenly, Gideon blew his trumpet and broke his pitcher. The torch blazed out. Three hundred trumpets began to blow. Three hundred pitchers broke. Three hundred torches blazed out.

The Midianites thought a huge army was attacking them; they were confused and afraid. They ran and ran as fast as they could. Soon all the Midianites had run away. "God has saved us from the Midianites," shouted Gideon.

Story based on Judges 6,7.

❦

Something to Think About: What did the Israelites and Gideon do when they were in trouble and thought God had forgotten them? Have you ever thought that God has forgotten you?

Illustration by Fred Schnaple, 1938

46

Samson

You would think that the Israelites would have learned their lesson, but it wasn't long until they were again worshiping false gods. This time God punished them by allowing the Philistines to conquer and rule them for forty years.

Then an angel of the Lord appeared to a woman who had been unable to have any children. The angel told her, "You are going to have a special son. He must never cut his hair or drink wine because he is to be dedicated to God."

When the child was born, he was named Samson, and he grew to be the strongest man in the land. With his bare hands he killed a lion.

The Philistines were always looking for ways to get rid of Samson. But with the strength God gave him, he defeated whoever came after him. Once he killed one thousand of them with just a donkey's jawbone used as a club.

Then he met a beautiful Philistine woman named Delilah. Samson began visiting her even though God warned him to stay away. But instead of praying for strength to obey God, he went right on seeing her.

Finally, Delilah got Samson to tell the secret of his strength. "I am a Nazirite," He explained. "I was dedicated to God at birth, that's why my hair has never been cut. If it were, God's strength would leave me."

So when Samson fell asleep, Delilah had his hair shaved off. Then she called in the Philistine soldiers to arrest him. When they charged into the room, Samson woke up and had no strength.

The Philistines put out Samson's eyes and then put him in prison and made him grind grain every day.

"Look at the great champion of Israel now!" the Philistines shouted. But God gave Samson another chance.

One day about three thousand Philistines were having a great feast in their temple when they decided to bring Samson in to laugh at him. But Samson asked the servant who was guiding him to lead him to the two main pillars that held up the roof of the temple. As he leaned against them, Samson prayed, "God, please give me back my strength just one more time, and let me die with the Philistines."

Then Samson pushed with all his might on the pillars, and the whole temple crashed down, killing everyone in it.

Story based on Judges 13—16.

❧

Something to Think About: How could Samson have saved his strength? What is something for which you need God's help in order to do what is right?

Illustration by Fred Schnaple, 1938

Ruth Finds a New Home

People all over Judah were hungry. It had not rained for a long, long time. The fields were brown and dry. There was no food for anyone to eat.

"We will go to another country," said Elimelech. "We will go where we can raise food to eat." So Elimelech and his wife Naomi went to live in Moab. Their two sons, Mahlon and Chilion, went with them.

For a while Elimelech's family was very happy. They liked to live in Moab. Mahlon and Chilion married beautiful Moabite girls. Their names were Ruth and Orpah.

One day Elimelech died. Then Mahlon and Chilion died. Naomi was left alone with Ruth and Orpah. They were all very sad.

At last Naomi began to think of her home in Judah. "I want to go back," she said. "The people in Judah love God. They love the God I love. The Moabites love their idols."

Ruth and Orpah loved Naomi. "We will go back with you," they said. "No," said Naomi. "You must stay here. You must go back to your homes. Then you will be happy again."

So Orpah went back to her home. But Ruth did not go. "Do not ask me to leave you," she said. "I want to go where you go. I want to love your God. I want to live with you and your people."

Naomi was thrilled. "Then we will go together," she said happily. So Ruth and Naomi walked together.

Illustration by Boecher, 1940

50

They went back to the land of Judah.

"Some of my family lives in Bethlehem," said Naomi. "We will go there." At last they came to Bethlehem. It was good to be home again. It was good to see grapevines. It was good to see fields of grain in the sun.

"Is this Naomi?" asked the people of Bethlehem. "We are glad you have come back. We are glad you brought Ruth. You will be happy living with us again."

The two women had arrived just as the barley harvest was beginning. And Naomi's relative, Boaz, welcomed Ruth to gather all the grain she needed from his fields. Naomi and Ruth were happy to be in Bethlehem. God had helped them find a new home.

Story based on Ruth 1,2.

❧

Pray: Dear Lord, help me to love You more than anything else, and help me to want to be with Your people like Ruth did.

God Calls Samuel

Elkanah and Hannah were sad. They had no children. Every year when they went to God's house, Hannah prayed, "O Lord, give us a baby to love. If You do, we will give him back to You to love and serve You."

One time when they were at God's house, Hannah prayed so long that Eli, the priest scolded her. "What are you doing?" he asked. "You must have been drinking strong wine."

"No," said Hannah. "I have been praying for God to give me a son. I have been telling God how sad I am."

Eli was sorry. "God will answer your prayer," he said.

And God did answer Hannah's prayer. Before a year went by, Hannah and Elkanah had a baby boy. How happy they were. Each day they thanked God. "His name will be Samuel," said Hannah.

Each year Samuel grew taller and stronger. At last it was time for him to go to God's house to stay.

Hannah was not sad this time when she went to God's house. "I am the woman who prayed for a boy," she told Eli. "God heard me and gave me Samuel. I want Samuel to stay in God's house and help you."

"God bless you," said Eli. "I cannot see well anymore, and I need someone to help me." So Samuel lived with Eli and helped him in God's house. And Eli taught him many things about God.

One night when Samuel went to bed he heard someone call, "Samuel." So he ran to Eli. "Here I am," he said.

"I didn't call you," said Eli. "Go back to bed."

Samuel went back to bed. But again he heard the voice calling. Samuel ran to Eli again. But Eli said, "I didn't call you, Samuel. Go back to bed."

"Samuel, Samuel," the voice came again. Samuel ran to Eli. "You *did* call me," he said.

Then Eli knew it was God. "God wants to talk to you, Samuel," said Eli. "If He calls again, answer Him."

Soon the voice called again, and Samuel said, "Speak, Lord, for I am listening."

So God talked with Samuel, then and in the years after.

Samuel became God's prophet. He loved God and God's people. Samuel helped them learn more about Him. "Samuel is a good prophet," said the people. "He helps us know what God wants us to do."

Story based on I Samuel 1—3.

❦

Something to Think About: How can you tell the Lord that you want to hear Him? What is one way the Lord speaks to us today?

Illustration by Elias Sallman, 1946

52

'We Want a King!'

U nlike other nations, Israel had never had a king. Instead of a king, God Himself had guided them through leaders like Moses, Joshua, and Samuel.

But one day some Israelites came to Samuel and said, "We want to be like the other nations. We want a king," they begged.

So Samuel agreed to pray about it.

"Don't be discouraged," God replied. "The people aren't rejecting you; they're rejecting Me. Samuel, you must grant their request. But first, warn them of what having a king will be like."

So Samuel told the people, "If you want a king, you may have one. But here's what your king will do: He will send your sons to war, make servants of your daughters, and feed your best crops to his own court."

But the people insisted, "We still want a king!" And so God allowed them to have their way.

In spite of the people's foolish decision, God continued to love and care for them. In fact, He even showed Samuel just who Israel's king should be.

One day a young farmer named Saul was trying to catch some stray donkeys, and he went to Samuel for help in finding them. That was when God told Samuel that Saul was to be Israel's king.

After receiving this message from God, Samuel invited Saul to a big feast. He seated Saul in the place of honor and treated him like true royalty.

"Why is he doing all of this for me?" Saul wondered.

Later Samuel told him. "Saul," he said, "God has chosen you to be the king of Israel." Saul couldn't believe he was hearing right!

To convince him that God had actually chosen him—and to prepare Saul for the work ahead of him—God showed Saul three miracles. In one of these miracles, the Spirit of God came upon him, changing his attitudes and giving him the ability to think wisely.

When Samuel first told the people that Saul had been chosen to be their king, most welcomed him and said, "Long live the king!" But a few of them laughed. Saul was just a farm boy!

But later, when one of Israel's cities was threatened by enemy Ammonites, Saul acted like a true king. Rallying the nation behind him, Saul defeated the Ammonites and rescued the city. Then Israel cheered the new king!

"But if you and your king turn away from God," Samuel warned, "you will know great hardship."

Story based on I Samuel 8—12.

❦

Something to Think About: Have you ever begged and begged for something your parents said wasn't good for you—like too much candy—until finally they gave it to you anyway? Afterwards, were you sorry when you felt sick?

Illustration by M. Wilhoite, 1944

54

God Chooses a Shepherd

Just as God had warned, King Saul placed heavy taxes on the people. Furthermore, after a time, he stopped obeying God.

"Saul is no longer a good king," God told Samuel. "He must be replaced. Go to Bethlehem and find the family of Jesse. The new king will be one of his sons."

When Samuel found Jesse and seven of his sons, he had each of them come before him. But each time God said, "Not this one."

At last Samuel asked, "Do you have any other sons?"

"Just one," said Jesse. "David is out in the fields taking care of the sheep, but he is only a boy."

"Send for him," said Samuel.

When David went before Samuel, God told Samuel, "This is the one." So Samuel lifted his horn of oil and poured some on David's head showing that he would be king.

David could hardly believe it. "Thank You, God," he said. "Let me serve You, and You only."

A short time later the Israelites were again fighting the Philistines, and David's brothers were part of the army.

"Take some food out to your brothers," said Jesse.

When David reached the camp where the soldiers stayed, he asked, "How is the battle going?"

Before anyone could answer, a shout rang out across the valley. There, on the other side, stood a giant yelling, "Send a man to fight me. If he kills me, the Philistines will leave. If I kill him, you will be our slaves."

David looked at the soldiers. They were afraid. "Why doesn't someone go out to fight this man?" asked David.

"Be quiet," one of the brothers said. "Are you trying to show off? No man can fight that giant."

But David would not be quiet. "I am not trying to show off," he said. "I will fight him."

When King Saul heard that, he put his big suit of armor on David. "I cannot fight with this," said David. "I must fight the way I know how, with my sling and God's help."

Goliath was angry. "Am I a dog that a boy comes out to fight me with a sling?" But David quietly put a stone in his sling. He whirled it 'round and 'round. The stone flew through the air and hit Goliath in the forehead. The giant fell to the ground, dead, and Israel was free.

Story based on I Samuel 16—17.

❧

Something to Think About: How could a mere boy kill a great giant? What was the secret of David's courage?

Illustration by M. Wilhoite, 1944

The Jealous King

David stood tall and straight as he marched to King Saul's tent. "You have saved our country from the Philistines," said King Saul. "I want to do something for you. You will come to live with me in my home. My son, Prince Jonathan, will be with you."

David smiled at Prince Jonathan. He knew at once that they would be friends.

"You killed the giant and helped our soldiers fight the enemy," said Prince Jonathan. "I am glad to be your friend." Before David knew what had happened, Jonathan took off his beautiful robe, his bow, and his sword and gave them to David.

David was very happy to have such a good friend. "I will be your friend all of my life," said David. David knew Jonathan was a true friend.

Then King Saul and Jonathan and David went back to the king's house. It was a day of great celebration. The giant Goliath had been killed, and the Philistine army had fled. Everyone poured out into the streets as Israel's army marched proudly home. The women cheered and danced for joy. They sang:

"Saul has slain his thousands,
And David his ten thousands."
Suddenly, King Saul realized that the people were saying better things about David than they were saying about him. He became very jealous.

Then he remembered the day that the prophet Samuel had come to him and said, "You have acted foolishly. You have not kept the command the Lord your God gave you. Therefore, your kingdom will be given to another."

"This must be the man," said Saul to himself. "I cannot let this happen."

So Saul began to plan how he might get rid of David. Several times he became so jealous that he went into a mad rage and threw his spear at David. But the Lord protected David.

At one point Saul made David a captain in his army and sent him to battle, hoping he would get killed. But the Lord went with David and blessed him in all his battles. And every time he got back to Israel, he was more popular than ever with the people.

King Saul's anger now knew no bounds. Everything he did to get rid of David failed. Saul realized that God was protecting David. But, instead of calming the king, this made him even more jealous. "I have to get rid of him!" Saul shouted. "I have to!"

Young David was in great danger. But God was with him. And Saul was powerless before God!

Story based on I Samuel 17:57—19:18.

❧

Pray: Thank You, God, that You will protect me like You did David if I will honor and obey You.

Illustration by Fred Schnaple, 1938

58

Solomon, the Wisest King

The years went by, and King Saul was killed by the Philistines. David became the new King. King David pleased God. Even though he sinned, he repented and asked God to forgive him.

During David's reign, Israel grew and prospered, and David worked for many years to build up the city of Jerusalem. It was very beautiful, but David was not happy. "There is one more building that must be built," he said. "We must have a temple for God."

But God would not let him build it. "You have killed too many people in wars," God told him. "You must let your son, Solomon, build My house when he becomes king."

Finally, David grew old and became sick. Some of the people were worried. "If King David dies, who will be king?" they asked.

While the people worried, David's oldest son, Adonijah, said, "Since I am the king's oldest son, I will become king."

But Zadok, the priest, heard what had happened. He went to see King David. "God told you which son would be king," he said. "Now Adonijah is making himself king. Is this what you want?"

King David knew he had waited too long. He should have made his younger son, Solomon, king to take his place.

So King David had Zadok pour oil on Solomon's head before a crowd of people. Then the people knew that Solomon was the man God had chosen to be king.

"God save King Solomon," they shouted. When Adonijah heard that, he ran to the altar where the people worshiped. He was afraid Solomon would kill him for trying to become king first. "I will not come out until you promise not to hurt me," he said.

Then Solomon told him, "If you are a good brother, no one will hurt you."

When David died, God talked to Solomon one day. "What would you like to have?" God asked him.

Solomon thought and thought. He could be rich and powerful. He could be famous. But finally Solomon said, "Let me be wise."

God was very pleased. "Since you have asked for the best gift for a king," God said, "you will not only be wise, you will also be rich and powerful."

So King Solomon became the wisest king on earth. And God let him build the beautiful temple in Jerusalem that was God's house for many years.

Story based on I Kings 1—9:5.

❧

Pray: Dear Lord, please help me to desire the best things in life which are not power and riches but the wisdom to obey You.

Illustration by Elias Sallman, 1945

Fire from Heaven

Years later, Ahab was the king of Israel, but he did not love God. Instead, he worshiped the idol Baal. And he let his wife, Jezebel, order God's special teachers (called prophets) put to death.

But one day God's prophet, Elijah, walked bravely into their throne room and said, "As surely as God lives," Elijah told the king, "there will be no rain until I say so."

Then Elijah left just as suddenly as he had come.

Elijah's words came true—there was no rain. The land became dry; the crops did not grow.

Jezebel ordered the soldiers to find Elijah and put him to death. But no one could find Elijah.

God had told Elijah, "Go to the brook called Cherith. I have commanded the ravens to bring you food."

Elijah obeyed God. He went to the brook where each morning and each evening the ravens brought him food.

Finally, Elijah sent a challenge to Ahab. "Tell all the priests of Baal and all the people to come to Mt. Carmel."

King Ahab was afraid because he knew Elijah was a man of God. So he did what Elijah said.

At Mt. Carmel Elijah stood in front of all the people. "How long will you try to worship two gods?" he asked. "If our God is really the true God, you should worship Him. If Baal is the true God, worship Him.

"Today we'll have a test," he said.

"Let the priests of Baal put some meat on an altar. Then I will put some meat on an altar. If Baal sends fire to burn the meat, he is the true God. If the Lord sends fire to burn the meat, He is God."

The people nodded their heads. "This is a good test," they said.

The priests of Baal danced around their altar. They cried louder and louder for Baal to hear them. But there was no fire.

Then Elijah built an altar with twelve big stones and put big pieces of meat on it. Then he had water poured on it three times until everything was soaked.

Finally, Elijah prayed. "O God, let these people know that You are God."

Suddenly fire flashed down from the sky. It burned up the meat, the wood, and the twelve stones.

The people threw up their hands. "The Lord is our God," they cried. "We will serve Him."

Story based on I Kings 17 and 18.

❧

Pray: O Lord, please help me to have the courage to worship and obey You even when it seems like everyone else has forgotten You.

Illustration by M. Wilhoite, 1944

62

Elijah Gets a Helper

King Ahab told the wicked Queen Jezebel how Elijah had defeated the prophets of Baal in the contest at Mt. Carmel. But this made Jezebel so angry that she swore that she would kill Elijah. Elijah got frightened and ran away from the work God wanted him to do. But God spoke to him. "Go back," God said, "for I will give you a helper."

Elijah started back, and along the way he saw a young man named Elisha. Elijah took off his coat and put it over Elisha's shoulders.

Elisha was surprised. "Does this mean I am to be a special messenger for God?" he asked.

Elijah nodded his head. "God has called you," he said.

So Elisha became Elijah's helper. Back in his own land Elijah spoke so bravely for God that even the wicked queen was afraid to harm him.

One day Elijah started off on a journey and Elisha went with him. Elisha knew Elijah would not come back and he wanted to be with him as long as he could.

Finally Elijah asked Elisha, "Is there anything you want to ask before God takes me away?"

"Yes," Elisha said. "Give me the power you have from God to do His work."

"If you see me when God takes me from you, it will be a sign that God has given the power to you," Elijah said.

And then a strange and wonderful thing happened! A chariot of fire drawn by horses of fire swept down between Elijah and Elisha. Elijah was lifted up into heaven by a whirlwind and his coat fell down in front of Elisha.

Elisha saw the horses and the chariot; he saw the whirlwind take Elijah from him.

Elisha picked up Elijah's coat. "O God," he prayed, "thank You for the gift of Your power."

And it was true. After this Elisha did many great miracles by the power of God. And he was one of the greatest prophets of Israel, and served God faithfully his whole life.

Story based on I Kings 19:19-21;
II Kings 2:1-15.

❧

Something to Think About: Where does power to do good come from? God may not ask you to do miracles, but where can you get the power to do good?

Illustration by R. Holberg, 1945

A Room for the Prophet

Whenever the prophet Elisha was traveling near the village of Shunem, he stayed with a couple who had built him a special room on the top of their house.

"You have been very kind to me," said Elisha one day when he was visiting. "What can I do for you?"

"We have plenty," said the woman.

Then Elisha's servant quietly suggested to Elisha, "She has no son and her husband is old."

That's it, thought Elisha, and he said to the woman, "About this time next year, you will have a baby son."

The woman did not think this was possible and said, "Please, Elisha, don't raise our hopes about something that can't happen."

As Elisha had prophesied, she had a baby. The boy grew and brought the couple much joy until one day he was out in the fields with his father. Suddenly he became very sick. "My head, my head," he said. Quickly the servants carried him back to the house.

The boy got worse, and by noon he died. In her grief, the woman carried the boy's body upstairs and laid it on the bed in Elisha's little room. Then she set out on a donkey to find Elisha.

She found him at Mount Carmel and told him of her great sorrow.

"Take my staff," said Elisha, "and run back home as fast as you can. Don't stop to talk to anyone, and when you get home, lay my staff on the boy's face."

But the Shunammite woman refused. "My grief is too great," she said. "I did not ask for our son, but you raised my hopes, and then God gave me one. Now I cannot stand to lose him. I'm not going to leave you."

So Elisha went with her back to her home. And there, in the little room, Elisha and his servant prayed.

Finally, the boy's body became warm. Then he sneezed seven times and opened his eyes.

The boy had come back to life.

The grateful mother threw her arms around her boy and was filled with great joy.

Story based on II Kings 4:8-37.

❧

Something to Think About: Why do you think the Shunammite woman did not want to go home alone without Elisha?

Illustration by Elias Sallman, 1945

A Brave Slave Girl

Naaman was the captain of the Syrian army. Syria was Israel's enemy to the north. From time to time bands of Syrians raided Israel taking captives for slaves. One of those slaves was a young Israelite girl who was sent to serve in the house of Naaman.

"What is wrong with Captain Naaman?" this little slave girl asked one day. "Why is he so sad?"

Captain Naaman's wife began to cry. "He has a terrible disease called leprosy," she said. "No one can help him."

The little slave girl shook her head. "But there is someone who can help him," she said. "His name is Elisha, a prophet of the true God in my home, Israel."

When Captain Naaman heard about Elisha, he asked his king to send him to Israel with a special letter. Perhaps Elisha could help him. He would see.

When the king of Israel read the letter from Naaman's king, he was angry and afraid. Naaman's king had forgot to ask for Elisha. "Who does your king think I am?" the king of Israel asked. "I cannot heal your leprosy."

The king of Israel worried and worried.

One day Elisha heard about Naaman. "Send him to me," he told the king.

So Naaman went to see Elisha. But before he could go into Elisha's house one of Elisha's servants met him.

Illustration by Richard Hook

68

"My master says you should wash seven times in the Jordan River," said the servant. "Then you will be healed."

Captain Naaman was angry. He did not want to wash in the muddy Jordan River. So he started to drive his chariot away.

"Wait," said one of his servants. "Elisha asked you to do something easy. Why not try it? Perhaps it may help."

Captain Naaman thought for a moment. Then he turned his chariot. He rode to the Jordan River.

Naaman looked at the muddy river. Why would this water help him? What would it do for him? Then he went down into the water. He dipped himself in the water seven times.

When Captain Naaman came out of the river, he could hardly believe his eyes. His spots were gone. He was healed. "Thank You, God," he said. "Thank You for Elisha. And thank You for the little girl who told me about Elisha."

Story based on II Kings 5:1-16.

❧

Something to Think About: What is one simple thing God wants you to do?

Jonah, the Runaway Prophet

Many years passed. Sometimes God's people were faithful, and sometimes they disobeyed, but God always cared for them by sending a prophet to remind them of God's ways and call the people back to Him.

But God loves all the people of the world, and He wants everyone to do what is right.

One day God spoke to Jonah. He was a prophet who lived in the northern kingdom of Israel. God told him, "Go to Nineveh. Tell the people to stop doing wrong or their city will be destroyed."

Jonah did not want to go to Nineveh. Not only was it a wicked city, but Nineveh was part of the great Assyrian Empire to the north. Assyria was even greater than Syria, and its armies threatened Israel. The soldiers in Nineveh were strong and very cruel.

"The people are wicked; they *should* be destroyed," Jonah said to himself. So, instead of doing what God told him to do, he ran away. He got on a ship that would take him to Tarshish, far away from Nineveh.

While the ship was at sea a terrible storm came up. The sailors were afraid. "What can we do?" they cried.

Jonah knew that the storm had come because he was trying to run away from God. "It's my fault," he said. "Throw me into the sea."

The sailors did, and a big fish swallowed Jonah. After three days God made the fish cast Jonah up on the shore.

Then God spoke again to Jonah. "Go to Nineveh. Tell the people to stop doing wrong or their city will be destroyed."

This time Jonah did not try to run away. Instead he said, "O God, forgive me for not obeying You. I will do what You say."

Jonah went to Nineveh and told the people: "You must change your ways or your city will be destroyed in forty days."

The people were afraid. They ran to the king and told him what Jonah had said. The king was afraid, too.

"Jonah is right," the king said. "We must stop being mean and selfish. Tell the people to pray to God and ask Him to forgive us."

The people *were* sorry; they asked God to forgive them and help them do right.

Jonah learned something wonderful: God loves people of *all* lands and He wants them to love and obey Him.

Story based on the Book of Jonah.

❦

Something to Think About: Can you think of someone who is so bad that it is hard to believe that God loves them? But what does this story tell us about God's love?

Illustration by Richard Hook

70

Good King Hezekiah Prays for Help

Even though God's prophets called the people to repent, the people and the kings of Israel continued to disobey God, worship idols, and treat each other badly. Finally, God allowed the Assyrian army to invade their land and take most of the people away as slaves. They were scattered so far that their nation never recovered.

But in the southern kingdom of Judah, there arose a good king who wanted to obey God.

Hezekiah was just a young man when he became king. As he looked around, he saw trouble everywhere.

My people are worshiping idols. They have forgotten God," Hezekiah said to himself. "Even the doors of the temple have been closed; the lamps are out. My people can never be happy until they turn back to God."

So, in the first month that he was king, he called the religious leaders to him. "Open the doors of the temple; clean it; light the lamps. Make it a place for people to worship God," he commanded.

Then good King Hezekiah and the rulers of the city went to God's house and asked Him to forgive their sins and help them obey Him always.

Because of Hezekiah's leadership, Judah enjoyed God's protection for many years. Once, when the Assyrian army tried to conquer Judah as it had Israel to the north, God destroyed the army and sent the Assyrian king fleeing back to Nineveh.

But in time Hezekiah became very sick. One day God's prophet, Isaiah, came to see him. Isaiah loved the king and wished he could give the king good news. But all he could say was, "I'm sorry, but you must get your things in order so that someone else can rule. You cannot get well."

Then Isaiah went away.

Hezekiah was so upset that he cried out: "O God, help me. I have tried to obey You in everything."

God heard Hezekiah's prayer, and He stopped Isaiah before he left the palace and sent him back.

Isaiah ran back to the king's room. "Good news," he cried. "God has heard your prayers and will make you well."

Then he told the servants to make a medicine from some figs for the king.

The servants obeyed. And King Hezekiah got well.

How happy the people were. And how happy Hezekiah was that he had obeyed God and that he could ask God for help.

Story based on II Chronicles 29 and II Kings 20:1-11.

❧

Pray: Dear Lord, thank You for always being there when I pray. Help me to obey you like good King Hezekiah did.

Illustration by Hockings, 1939

72

God's Book Is Found

Some of the kings of Judah were not good. They allowed idol worship. Then, a small boy was crowned king. His name was Josiah and he was only eight years old.

King Josiah wanted so much to be the kind of king that would please God. He wanted to do something special for God. So when he grew up into a young man, Josiah told his people they should fix God's house.

One day the king's helper, named Shaphan, went to see God's house. He talked with the priest, Hilkiah, about making God's house beautiful again.

Then Hilkiah showed Shaphan something he had found. "Look!" he said. "I found this large roll with writing on it. I found it while men were fixing God's house. It is the lost book of the Law."

Shaphan was excited. He took the Book and read some of it. In the Book were the laws God had given. Shaphan hurried to show the lost Book to King Josiah.

Josiah was so happy to know that God had given such a book. He had never seen one before.

"Read some of the Book to me," he said. Shaphan began to read from God's Book. The king listened carefully. He had never heard such wonderful things.

"But we are not living the way God wants," he said. Then Josiah prayed, "Forgive us, O God, for not doing what You want. Help me teach my people to obey Your laws every day of their lives."

Then Josiah called some men to him. "Go everywhere in the land," he said. "Tell all the people to come here to Jerusalem."

When all the people came to Jerusalem, Josiah went with them to God's house. Then he stood up before the people. He read to them from God's Book.

When Josiah stopped, he talked to the people. "I will do what God says in His Book," he said. "I want you to do what God says, too."

So the king made the people promise to do what God said. And for all the years that King Josiah ruled, the people did obey God.

King Josiah was so happy that the lost Book had been found. Now they knew what God wanted and they could do it!

Story based on II Chronicles 34; II Kings 22, 23.

❦

Something to Think About: Why do you think Josiah thought God's Book was so important? Do you think it is important to read God's Book?

Illustration by Fred Schnaple, 1935

74

Jeremiah and the Angry King

Again God's people were in trouble. They would not listen to God. They would not obey Him. They had returned again and again to idol worship. Though some kings obeyed God, others were very evil. They killed God's prophets and were very cruel to each other.

So God chose Jeremiah to speak to the people for Him. "I will help you," God told him. "I will tell you what to say."

God did tell Jeremiah what to say. He told him that the people must obey God. If they did not, enemy soldiers would come. They would burn their cities and take the people away.

The people of Judah knew that this same tragedy had happened to Israel, the northern kingdom, almost one hundred years before. But they did not think it would happen to them. So they did not believe Jeremiah, and they refused to obey God.

Then one day enemy soldiers *did* come. This time they came from Babylon, a mighty empire to the east. They attacked and defeated the city of Jerusalem. They did not destroy the city, but they took many of the best young men back to Babylon with them. One of these young men was named Daniel. And he became an important prophet for God while living in Babylon.

Illustration by M. Wilhoite, 1947

76

But in Judah, God's people still had not repented. The prophet Jeremiah talked to a young man named Baruch. He told him to write some words on a roll of paper.

After Baruch wrote down the words, he read them to the people.

"You are in trouble because you do not obey God," he said.

The people listened. Some ran to tell the king.

When the king heard the words that Jeremiah had written, he was angry. He began cutting the roll into pieces. Then he threw the pieces into the fire.

"Put Jeremiah and Baruch in prison," the king shouted.

But God had already warned Jeremiah and Baruch so they could hide. Then the Lord spoke to Jeremiah again and said, "Take another roll of paper and write on it all the words that were on the first roll. Say that more punishment is coming. And if the king and the people do not repent, their land will certainly be destroyed."

Jeremiah bravely did exactly what God told him to do. But his message made everyone very angry, and Jeremiah was finally put into prison.

Story based on Jeremiah 36.

❦

Something to Think About: Why did Jeremiah's prophecy make the king and the people so angry? Why did Jeremiah continue preaching and writing down God's message? Have you ever tried to tell your friends what was right to do but it made them angry?

Daniel and His Friends

As punishment for Judah's sin, God allowed many people to be captured by their enemies and taken to Babylon.

Daniel and his friends were among those taken from Jerusalem to be slaves to a new king.

"King Nebuchadnezzar had a dream," the captain of the king's guard told them. "But he forgot what he dreamed. He wants to know what the dream meant. He asked magicians, but they could not tell him. The king became so angry that he ordered them killed."

"Let me talk with the king," said Daniel. "Perhaps I can help him."

When Daniel met with the king, God helped Daniel remind the king what he had dreamed. "You saw a big statue," said Daniel. "It had a head made of gold and feet made of clay. But a big stone rolled over and hit the statue. It fell and broke into pieces."

"Yes, yes," said the king. "That was it. But what does it mean?"

"Many kingdoms will fall like the statue," said Daniel. "But someday God will make a kingdom that will never fall."

"You have a great God," said the king. "I will make you ruler over all my court helpers."

But the magicians who did not believe in God were very angry. They did not like Daniel and his friends— Shadrach, Meshach, and Abednego. Finally, they came up with a plan to get rid of them.

Illustration by M. Wilhoite, 1944

78

"The king has said that everyone must worship his golden statue," they said. "Those who do not will be thrown into a fiery furnace."

They planned to watch Shadrach, Meshach, and Abednego because they knew that these Hebrews would not worship an idol. So the next day when the trumpet blew the magicians watched. When Shadrach, Meshach, and Abednego did not bow down before the king's statue, the magicians ran to tell the king.

The king was very angry. "Heat the furnace seven times hotter than before," he shouted. "Then tie up these men, and throw them into the fire."

But when Nebuchadnezzar's men threw Daniel's three friends into the fire, they were amazed. Shadrach, Meshach, and Abednego walked around in the furnace with a fourth person who looked like the son of God.

"Come out, come out," shouted the king. For the king knew then that their God had saved them.

"If anyone says anything against the God of Shadrach, Meshach, and Abednego," said the king, "he will die."

Story based on Daniel 2 and 3.

❧

Something to Think About: Why couldn't the magicians tell the king what he had dreamed? Is there any other way to gain true wisdom except from God?

Daniel in the Lions' Den

The captives from Jerusalem lived in Babylon for many, many years. Daniel served in the courts of the kings who followed Nebuchadnezzar. One of them was Darius.

King Darius was pleased with Daniel because he was honest and always did the right thing. So King Darius put Daniel in charge over all the princes of Babylon. But this made the princes hate him.

Like Nebuchadnezzar's magicians who wanted to get rid of Daniel's three friends, the princes in King Darius's court plotted how they could get rid of Daniel.

"If Daniel would do something wrong," they reasoned, "then we could trap him."

But Daniel didn't do wrong things. He always asked God to show him what to do. He prayed to God three times each day.

One day the princes came up with a plan. "King Darius," they said. "Make a law that everyone must worship only you for thirty days. Whoever does not will be thrown into a den of lions."

The king, who liked Daniel, did not know that the princes were trying to trap Daniel. So he signed the law. He liked the idea of everyone in the land worshiping him.

But the next day when Daniel prayed to God, the princes told the king. Then the king was sorry that he had made the foolish law. But once

Illustration by Baim, 1948

80

he had made a law, not even he could break it. So he had to have his friend Daniel thrown into a den of lions. And he said, "May your God, whom you always serve, save you."

All that night the king worried and could not sleep. The next morning he ran to the lions' den.

"Daniel, Daniel," called the king. "Did your God take care of you?"

"Yes," said Daniel. "He sent His angel and closed the mouths of the lions. They have not hurt me."

The king was very happy and ordered that Daniel be lifted out of the lions' den. But he also ordered that the evil men who had trapped Daniel be thrown into the lions' den. The lions were so hungry that they ate the men immediately.

Then Darius made another law. "All of my people will honor Daniel's God, for He is above all other gods."

So, for the rest of his life, Daniel helped to rule the land of Babylon. And Daniel never forgot to pray and ask for God's help.

Story based on Daniel 6.

❦

Something to Think About: How do you think Daniel felt when the king told all the people to worship the true God?

Going Home

God's people, the Jews, were captives in Babylon for seventy years. During this time they finally learned to obey God much better.

When Daniel was very old, God arranged for His people's punishment to be over and for them to return to Judah. One day King Cyrus issued the following order: "All Jews who want to return to their own country may do so."

How exciting! The Jewish people could go home at last! But some, like Daniel, were too old to make the nine-hundred-mile trip. Others had set up businesses in Babylon and didn't want to leave them.

Finally, about fifty thousand Jews made the long journey. They were thrilled to be in the land of Judah again. Children who had never seen Jerusalem—but had heard much about it—were excited to walk around at last in the capital city.

The people set to work to rebuild the city and the temple. When the temple was finally completed, the people decided to celebrate the Passover—the time when God brought them out of Egypt. What a celebration it was! "We have never had a happier Passover!" the people said to each other.

Ezra was not in the first group of Jews to return to Jerusalem. He was a scribe, a man who studied and taught God's law.

About eighty years after the Jews first returned to Jerusalem, Ezra met a traveler in Babylon who had just come from there. Eagerly, Ezra asked, "How are things in Jerusalem?"

The man replied, "The walls around the city are still not repaired. The temple was rebuilt, but now it's being neglected. People in Judah don't seem to know God's law. They don't have anybody to teach them."

"How can that be?" Ezra wondered. "Even in Babylon the Jews are taught God's law! I need to go to Jerusalem myself to teach the people."

Ezra set out for Jerusalem with another large group of Jewish companions. It was a good trip. They were only on the road about four months. "The people will listen to me," Ezra thought as he walked.

They did listen! Ezra taught the law again to the people. He encouraged them to confess their sins and follow God exactly.

Ezra also led the people to work and cooperate together. Ezra praised God and gave Him all the credit for the good things that happened in Jerusalem.

Story based on Ezra 1—3 and 6.

❧

Pray: Dear Lord, thank You for Your forgiveness and help as we return to You and want to do as You teach.

Illustration by Fred Schnaple, 1935

Queen Esther

Esther was one of the Jews who did not return from Babylon to Judah. She was an orphan who lived with her Uncle Mordecai in Persia.

The Persian palace was filled with excitement. The king was looking for a new queen. Lovely girls were gathered from throughout the land to see whom the king would choose.

Esther was one of these girls, and when the king saw her, he chose her as his new queen.

One day a servant told Esther that her Uncle Mordecai was very upset and was pacing back and forth in front of the palace.

Esther immediately sent a messenger to find out what was wrong. The answer was, "The king has ordered all the Jews in Persia to be killed."

Mordecai sent word to Esther that the king's assistant, Haman, was angry because everyone except Mordecai bowed when he passed. Mordecai would not bow, and Haman had persuaded the king to kill the Jews. "Please speak to the king."

"I don't dare," said Esther. "Nobody can go before the king without an invitation—not even the queen. The penalty can be death."

"You must go," her uncle insisted. "Perhaps God made you queen so you could save your people."

"Then pray for me," said Esther. "I will try."

After praying for three days, Esther entered the throne room. She waited, watching the king's face. "What can I do for you?" the king asked.

Esther did not answer right away. Instead, she said, "I would like to invite you and Haman to a banquet I have prepared."

"We will come," replied the king.

At the banquet, Esther still did not tell what she really had on her mind. Instead, she invited them to another dinner the next night.

The next evening, when the king had finished eating his dinner, he turned to Queen Esther and said, "This is wonderful. What can I do for you? Whatever you want, up to half the kingdom, I will give you."

Then Esther said, "If I have pleased you, your majesty, please save me and my people. For we are to be killed."

"What?" demanded the king. "Who would do this?"

Pointing to Haman, Esther said, "He has plotted to kill us all! For I am a Jew."

The king ordered Haman to be hanged on the very gallows that Haman had built for Mordecai, and the Jews were spared.

Story based on Esther 1—7.

Something to Think About: What gave Esther the courage to risk her life for the sake of her people? When you need help doing a hard thing, where can you find it?

Illustration by Baim, 1948

84

"Jesus did many other things as well. If every one of them were written down, I suppose that even the whole world would not have room for the books that would be written."

John 21:25, NIV

New Testament

The Promise of a Savior-King

Whenever the sin of the people got them into great trouble, God always sent a prophet to encourage them to repent and return to Him. The prophets often promised that God would one day rescue them Himself.

The prophet Isaiah said, "A virgin will have a Son, and His name will be called 'God with us.' He will judge with fairness and care for His people like a good Shepherd. Tell Jerusalem that her salvation is coming."

The prophet Jeremiah said, "That Savior-King will sit on David's throne forever."

The prophet Daniel said, "All people, all nations will serve Him."

And the prophet Micah said, "He shall be born in the little town of Bethlehem."

These and many other promises comforted the people in their suffering.

Mary lived hundreds of years after these prophecies had been given. She was a godly girl and believed that God would someday fulfill His promise. But she did not know when.

Every day when she went to get water from the well she listened to other people talk about the wonderful promise that God had made to His people.

"God will send a strong and brave King," they said. "He will drive away the bad men who rule us."

Mary thought and thought about this Savior-King. "I wish I could talk to my cousin Elisabeth," she said to herself. "She knows God's Word so well. I wonder when she thinks God will send the Savior-King?"

Mary often prayed that God would send the King.

One day, while Mary was praying, she looked up to see an angel standing near her. Mary had never seen an angel before. She was afraid. She did not know what to do.

"Don't be afraid," the angel whispered. "I have good news for you. God has sent me to tell you that you will be the mother of the Savior-King. He will be God's Son."

Mary looked at the angel. "How wonderful," she whispered. "God wants me to be the mother of His Son."

"You will call His name Jesus," said the angel. "He will rule for ever and ever."

Mary closed her eyes. "Thank You, God," she prayed. "Thank You for letting me be the mother of Your Son, the Savior-King."

"I *must* go visit Elisabeth," Mary thought. "She must hear my news."

When Mary finally arrived at Elisabeth's house, Elisabeth said, "God bless you for believing what the Lord told you."

Story based on Luke 1:26-38.

❧

Something to Think About: When God promises something, does it always come true? What if you have waited many, many years; will it still happen?

Illustration by Joe Tillotson, 1949

88

The Shepherds

Joseph loved Mary and wanted to marry her. But when he discovered that she was already going to have a baby, he couldn't understand because he wasn't the father. So the angel came to Joseph in a dream and said, "Don't worry. The baby inside Mary is a miracle from God. You are to name Him Jesus, because He will be the Savior-King."

So Joseph married Mary and took her with him when he had to travel to his parents' hometown of Bethlehem to pay taxes.

One night the shepherds in the hills around Bethlehem were standing around their fire watching their sheep and the lights of the little town below.

"Nothing much is happening tonight," said one of the shepherds. "Nothing much ever happens," said another. "Even the wolves have not come around for a while."

Suddenly there was a bright light around the shepherds. The light was shining from the sky. In the light was an angel. They had never seen anything like this before.

The shepherds were afraid. Then the angel spoke to them. "Don't be afraid," he said. "I have something good to tell you. God's Son has been born in Bethlehem."

The shepherds looked at each other. "In Bethlehem!" they said. "God's Son born tonight?"

The angel went on. "You will find the Baby lying in a manger." Then all at once many, many angels came in the sky. "Glory to God in the highest," they said. "Peace to men on earth." Then the angels were gone.

The shepherds looked at each other. Angels had come to see them in the lonely fields. Never before had such a thing happened. And the angels had told them of God's Son, born this very night in the little town below them.

"Hurry," the shepherds said to each other. "Let's go see what has happened."

So the shepherds hurried into Bethlehem. There they found the Baby, just as the angels had said.

The shepherds looked at the little Baby. They whispered quietly to each other. "This is God's Son! What good news the angels brought to us!"

The shepherds were so happy that they told everyone they saw about the new Baby. They told about the angels and the good news. But most of all, the shepherds thanked God for sending His Son to Bethlehem, for this was a night like no other night.

Story based on Matthew 1:18-25 and Luke 2:1-7.

❦

Pray: Thank You, God, for sending Your Son to be our Savior-King.

Illustration by Richard Hook

90

Wise Men from Afar

In a land far away, Wise Men were watching the sky one night. Suddenly one of them pointed up at the stars.

"Look at that star," he said. "It is brighter than all of the others."

The other Wise Men looked at the bright star. They could not take their eyes from it.

"It is a sign from God," they said. "It is God's way to tell us that His great King has been born. Now we must leave here and go to see Him."

So the Wise Men took gifts and food. They rode on their camels for many days. They talked about the King who had been born far away.

When they got to Jerusalem they went to see King Herod and said, "We have come to worship the new King. We saw His star in the east from our home. Where is He?"

King Herod did not know about the birth of Jesus. He was wicked and afraid that a new king might remove him from his throne. So he called all the Bible teachers and asked them where the prophecies said the Savior-King was to be born. "The prophet Micah said He would be born in Bethlehem," they said.

So Herod sent the Wise Men to Bethlehem, saying, "When you find this new King, come back and tell me so that I can go and worship Him."

When the Wise Men got to Bethlehem, they saw the bright star again. It led them until they found a little house.

Illustration by Dalrymple, 1938

"We have found the great King at last," they said. "He is here in this house."

Inside the house the Wise Men did find the great King. They found Mary with the baby Jesus.

The Wise Men bowed down before the baby Jesus. They gave Him the gifts they had brought. They gave Him gold, frankincense, and myrrh.

"How did you know the Baby was here?" Mary asked the Wise Men.

So the Wise Men told of the star that God had sent. "It was God's sign that a king was born," they said.

Mary thought of the things the Wise Men had said. She knew that God had many wonderful ways to tell others about His Son.

God warned the Wise Men not to tell Herod about Jesus because Herod planned to kill Him. So they went home a different way.

Story based on Matthew 2:1-12.

❧

Something to Think About: Why do you think Herod wanted to kill Jesus?

92

The Flight to Egypt

Joseph and Mary were the happiest people in all Bethlehem. God had chosen Mary to be the mother of His Son. And He had told Joseph to take care of them. Joseph was glad to do this because he loved God, and he loved Jesus and Mary.

But one night Joseph had a dream. And in the dream an angel spoke to him.

"Get up!" the angel said. "Get up quickly. Take Jesus to Egypt, for King Herod wants to kill Him. Stay in Egypt until I tell you it is safe to return."

Joseph got up at once. He called to Mary and told her what the angel said.

Mary was frightened. "Why?" she cried. "Why would a big, powerful king want to harm a tiny baby?" She held her baby close.

"I don't know," Joseph said, "but God knows what the king plans to do."

So, as fast as he could, Joseph packed their things on the back of their little donkey. Mary wrapped little Jesus in a soft blanket. Then, while it was still dark, they hurried out of the city.

It was a long way to Egypt, and often on the way Joseph and Mary asked themselves, "When will it be safe for us to return home?"

Illustration by Hockings, 1939

Joseph was a good carpenter, and down in Egypt he got a job. He took care of Mary and Jesus. Then, one night, he had another dream. Again, the angel came to him. "The king who wanted to kill Jesus is dead," the angel said. "It is safe now for you to take Jesus home."

So, once again, Joseph and Mary did what the angel told them to do. They packed their things and went back to their own land.

How glad they were to be home. But Joseph had another dream in which God warned him that it was still not safe to live in Judea. Herod's son was on the throne, and he might also want to harm the child. So Joseph and Mary and Jesus went north and settled in the town of Nazareth of Galilee.

How glad Joseph and Mary were that God had helped them take care of Jesus.

Story based on Matthew 2:13-15, 19-23.

❧

Pray: Dear Lord, when my family has to move or when I have to make other big changes in my life, please help me to trust You.

The Boy Jesus at the Temple

Every year Mary and Joseph traveled from Nazareth down to Jerusalem to observe the Feast of the Passover. It was a long trip and took several days of travel by foot.

Jesus was excited. It was the time of year to make the special trip with his mother and father. Many of His friends and relatives made the trip together, walking and playing along the way, and singing and telling stories by the campfire at night. Jesus loved to sleep out under the stars at night. But most important was the Passover and the time they would spend at the temple in Jerusalem.

When the people came to Jerusalem, they went to the temple to worship. Jesus went, too. He liked to visit God's house. He liked to hear the teachers talk about God.

The Feast of the Passover lasted seven days as the people worshiped God and remembered His great deliverance of their ancestors from Egypt. But at last it was time to go home. Mary and Joseph left Jerusalem with their friends. It was a large group of people that started out on the dusty road returning to the towns and villages north of Jerusalem.

After they had traveled some distance, Mary asked Joseph, "Where is Jesus? I haven't seen Him all day."

"I don't know. I thought He was with some friends or relatives," Joseph answered.

Mary and Joseph looked everywhere. But Jesus was not among any of the travelers.

Finally, they turned back toward Jerusalem. "Have you seen a twelve-year-old boy named Jesus?" they asked everyone they met along the way. But no one had seen Jesus.

At last, after three days, they went back to the temple, and there they saw Him, talking with the teachers in God's house. The teachers were surprised to hear how much Jesus knew about God.

"We have been worried about You," Mary told Jesus.

But Jesus answered, "Didn't you know I would be here in My Father's house?"

After Jesus said good-bye to the teachers, He went back to Nazareth with Joseph and Mary and was obedient to them. There He grew tall and strong. Everyone loved Jesus. And God loved Him, too.

Story based on Luke 2:41-52.

❦

Something to Think About: Why do you think Jesus was talking with the teachers at the temple? Why did Jesus call the temple His "Father's house"?

Illustration by Winter, 1938

96

John the Baptist

When Jesus was a grown man, His cousin, John, began preaching in the desert of Judea. John dressed in rough clothes made of camel's hair with a leather belt around his waist. He ate what wild food he could find—grasshoppers and wild honey.

He preached from the Old Testament Book of Isaiah and told people to repent from their sins because the Lord's Messiah was coming soon. People came from the city of Jerusalem and all the surrounding towns to hear him preach. Many people repented, and to express their sorrow for having disobeyed God and to show that they wanted to change, they asked John to baptize them in the Jordan River.

But when the religious leaders came out to hear John, he spoke harshly to them because they were evil. Instead of repenting as they should have, they continued to sin, and worse, they boasted that God had to accept them anyway because they were part of God's people, the Jews.

John warned them that soon God's special Servant was coming who would judge everyone who hadn't repented of their sin.

One day Jesus came down from Galilee to visit John in the desert. He asked John to baptize Him. John, being Jesus' cousin, knew that Jesus lived a holy life, so he said, "Jesus, You are the One who ought to baptize me rather than me baptizing You."

But Jesus said, "No. You must baptize Me."

As soon as Jesus came up out of the water, the Spirit of God came down from heaven and landed on Jesus like a dove. And a voice from heaven said, "This is my Son, whom I love. With You I am well pleased."

John knew something very special had happened, and he started to understand that Jesus was the Messiah, the very Savior-King he had been telling people that God would soon send.

Story based on Matthew 3 and John 1:32-35.

❧

Pray: Dear Lord, help me to be quick to repent from my sin so that I can please You.

Illustration by Fred Schnaple, 1937

98

Jesus and the Four Fishermen

The people kept pushing. "I cannot hear what Jesus is saying," a man said, so he pushed a little harder.

"Now I cannot see Jesus," said the woman who had been pushed away.

Jesus knew what the trouble was. The crowd was so large that people couldn't see over one another or hear Him very well. So He got into a boat that belonged to a man named Simon. "Take your boat out a little way into the water," Jesus said.

Simon did. Then, when all of the people could see and hear Him, Jesus told them about God and how God wanted them to live.

When He finished He turned to Simon and said, "Take your boat out into deep water and let down your nets. Then you will get some fish."

Simon shook his head sadly. "We have fished all night and caught nothing. But if You say so, we will try again."

So Simon and his brother, Andrew, did as Jesus said. The nets became so full of fish that they began to break.

"Help us," they shouted to their friends, James and John. So James and John brought their boat over, and soon they had both boats so full of fish that they were about to sink.

They were all so surprised they did not know what to say or do. But Peter fell down on his knees in front of Jesus. "Go away from me," he said to Jesus. "For I am not good enough to be with One like You."

Illustration by Zingaro, 1943

100

Jesus looked at Peter in His kindly way. "Do not be afraid, Peter," He said. "From now on you will catch men."

The four fishermen believed Jesus; nothing was more important now than to be with Jesus. So they left their boats and followed Him.

Story based on Luke 5:1-11.

❧

Something to Think About: How was Jesus able to know where all the fish were when the experienced fishermen hadn't been able to catch any all night? Do you think Jesus knows what's best for your life?

Jesus Changes Water into Wine

One day Jesus and His followers were invited to a wedding in the town of Cana in Galilee. During the celebration—which lasted several days—the wine ran out.

It was embarrassing for the bridegroom to not have enough refreshments for his guests, so Jesus' mother asked Jesus to do something. But Jesus said, "Why do you ask Me to help? It's not the right time for Me to make Myself known."

Still, Jesus' mother, Mary, believed that He could help, so she told the servants, "Do whatever Jesus tells you to do."

Standing nearby were six huge water jars made of stone. Each could hold twenty to thirty gallons, more than enough water for a full bath.

Finally, Jesus told the servants to fill these stone jars with water. So they did. They filled them to the brim.

Then Jesus said, "Now, draw some out and take it to the head waiter of the banquet."

So they did, and when the head waiter tasted it, it was wine, not water. Jesus had turned the water into wine.

Now, the servants knew that the wine had been created by a miracle that Jesus had performed, but the head waiter did not know this, so he

Illustration by M. Wilhoite, 1947

called the bridegroom aside and said to him, "This is very strange. Everyone usually serves the best wine first, and then when everyone has had enough to drink, they bring out the cheaper wine, thinking the guests won't notice. But you have saved the best till now."

But the bridegroom hadn't provided the good wine, Jesus had. It was His first miracle in Cana of Galilee. And when His disciples saw it, it caused them to believe in Him.

Story based on John 2:1-11.

❦

Pray: O Lord, help me to be quick to obey You when You ask me to do something for You.

Through the Roof

Jesus will help you," some friends told the sick man. "We will take take you to Him."

The sick man could not walk. So his friends carried him on his bed. They took him through the streets of town. They took him to the house where Jesus was teaching.

But when they came to the house they could not get in. There were too many people. Everyone wanted to see Jesus.

"What shall we do?" one of the friends asked. "We'll never get through that crowd."

"Then let's go over the crowd," said another friend. "We'll go up on the roof and let our friend down through the roof to see Jesus."

The friends picked up the bed with the sick man on it. They climbed up some outside stairs to the roof of the house. Then, slowly and carefully, they took some parts of the roof off. They tied ropes to the four corners of their friend's bed and let the sick man down through the hole in the roof.

Slowly and gently the bed came right down into the middle of the crowd, right by Jesus. Jesus looked at the man who had come down through the roof. Then He smiled.

"Your sins are forgiven," Jesus said.

Some of the Jewish leaders were upset. "Only God can forgive sins. Who does this Man think He is?"

But Jesus knew what they were thinking, so He said, "You are right. Only God can forgive sins. Therefore,

Illustration by Richard Hook

104

I will show you that I can forgive sins." Then Jesus turned to the sick man and said, "Stand up!"

The man did not know what to do. He couldn't walk. But Jesus was telling him to stand up. He did so.

Then Jesus said, "Pick up your bed and walk."

So the man did what Jesus said. He picked up his bed, and to everyone's surprise he began to walk.

"Thank You, thank You," the man told Jesus.

He walked out of the house and down the street toward home.

All the people watched the man walk. "Thank God," they said. "Thank God that Jesus can make us well again."

Story based on Luke 5:17-26.

❧

Something to Think About: When Jesus forgave the man's sins and healed him, what did it show about who Jesus is?

The Man Who Came to Jesus at Night

Nicodemus was a very important man. He was a ruler of the Jews and he was very rich. But he had a big problem. He wanted to talk to Jesus, but he was afraid that the other rulers would make trouble for him if he did. The other rulers did not believe that Jesus was God's Son. They did not want people to listen to Jesus because they might follow Jesus instead of them.

Nicodemus thought and thought about his problem. Finally he just *had* to see Jesus. So he waited until after dark, then he went to see Jesus.

"We know that You are a teacher who has come from God, for no one could do the things You do without God being with You," Nicodemus said to Jesus.

Jesus knew that Nicodemus wanted to learn more about God and His kingdom, and He wanted to help him. "You must be born again to enter God's kingdom," Jesus said.

"Born again?" Nicodemus asked. He could not understand what Jesus meant. "How can a man be born after he has grown up?" he asked.

Jesus did not mean that a man must get a new body; He meant that a man must get a new heart—one that is kind and loving and forgiving as God is.

Illustration by Richard Hook

For only a person who loves and obeys God can live forever with God.

Then Jesus told Nicodemus the most wonderful news in all the world: God loves the world so much that He sent His only Son to show people the way they can be a part of God's kingdom. And those who believe in God's Son will live forever with God.

Jesus wanted Nicodemus to live in God's kingdom. He wants us to live there, too. We can—if we believe in Jesus and try to do what He taught us.

Story based on John 3:1-21.

❦

Something to Think About: How can someone be born again?

106

The Woman at the Well

Jesus was tired so He sat down to rest at a well near a town in Samaria. In a few minutes a woman came to the well. But she did not speak to Jesus because Jesus was a Jew, and the Jews did not like the people of Samaria.

However, when she lifted a jar of water up from the well, Jesus said, "Give me a drink."

She was surprised. "You are a Jew," she said. "Why do you ask me, a woman of Samaria, to give you a drink?"

"If you knew who asked you for a drink you would ask Him to give you living water," Jesus said.

"Living water?" she asked. Now she was even more surprised, for she did not know that Jesus was talking about the wonderful gift of salvation. (This means that if we believe in Jesus He will save us from our sins so that we can live forever with God.)

Then Jesus talked to her about God, and how important it was for people to worship Him.

The woman nodded her head. "Someday God's chosen One will come," she said. "And when He comes He will tell us all things."

"I am that One for whom you wait," Jesus said.

God's chosen One—talking to her!

Illustration by Boecher, 1943

She could hardly believe that such a wonderful thing would happen to her. She must tell her friends. So she ran at once into the town and told the wonderful news to everyone she met.

The people hurried out to see Jesus. And, oh, how eagerly they listened as Jesus talked to them about God.

"Please stay and tell us more," the people begged. So Jesus stayed with the people of Samaria for two days; and many of them believed in Him.

How glad they were that Jesus loved them and that He wanted to share God's love with them.

Story based on John 4:3-43.

❦

Something to Think About: Who does Jesus love? To whom will He give God's gift of salvation?

Jairus's Daughter

The little girl in the big house was very, very sick. "Shhh," her father Jairus told everyone. "We must be very quiet for her."

Everyone was very quiet. They were quiet until one day a servant came running in. He was calling for Jairus.

When Jairus came running, the servant began to talk. "I have good news," he said. "Jesus is here in town. He can make your little girl well."

Jairus ran out the door and down the street. He ran everywhere, looking for Jesus. At last he found Him.

"Please come," said Jairus. "My little girl is so sick that she's going to die. But I know You can heal her."

Jesus looked at Jairus. He felt sorry for him. "I will go with you," He said.

As Jesus walked through the crowds toward Jairus's house, a woman who had been sick for several years reached out and touched the edge of Jesus' robe. Immediately, she was healed.

"Who touched me?" said Jesus.

"Master," said Peter, who was walking with Him, "there are so many people around You, anybody could have touched You."

Then the woman who had been healed, kneeled before Jesus and admitted that she had been the one who had reached out for help from Jesus.

"That's fine," said Jesus. "Your faith has healed you. Go in peace."

Then as Jesus and Jairus and the others continued on, a servant came running from Jairus's house. The man looked very sad.

"You are too late," he said. "The little girl is dead."

Jairus was very, very sad. He loved his little girl so much. If only Jesus hadn't been delayed on the way, He could have healed her.

"Don't be sad," Jesus told him. "I will help you."

Jairus believed Jesus. He knew that Jesus could do anything.

When Jesus came into the big house, He took the little girl by the hand. "Little girl," He said, "stand up."

The little girl opened her eyes. She stood up as Jesus told her to do.

Jairus was the happiest man in the world. He hugged his little girl. "Isn't Jesus wonderful?" he whispered.

Story based on Luke 8:40-56.

❧

Something to Think About: How do you think Jairus felt when Jesus got delayed on the way to help his daughter? Tell about one time when you had to wait for something good.

Illustration by Richard Hook

110

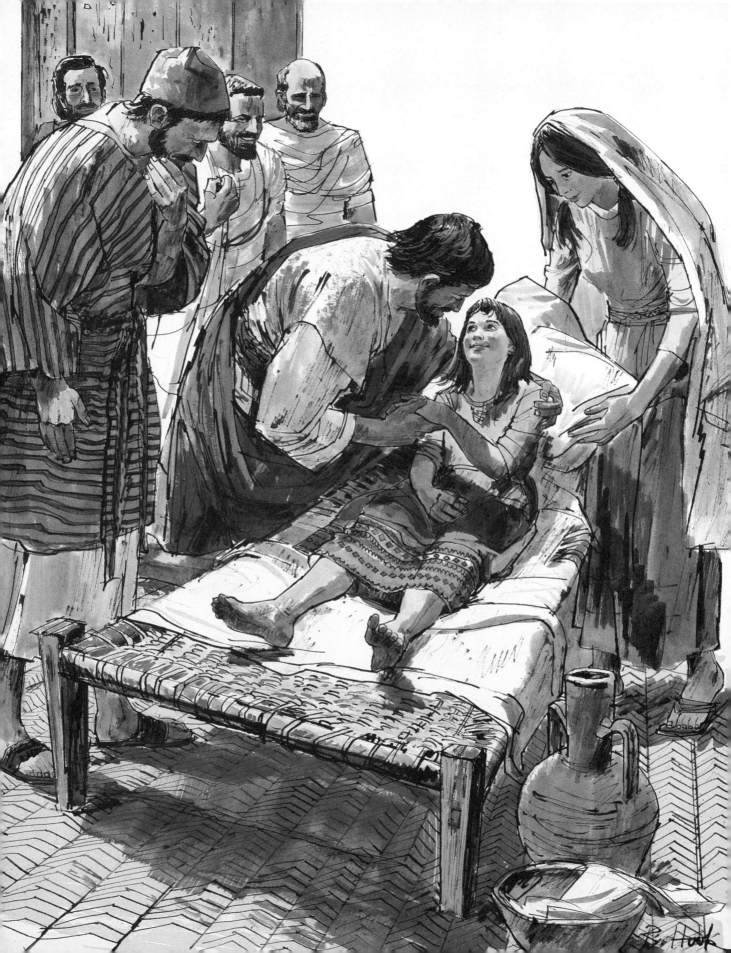

Jesus Heals the Deaf Man

The boys and girls stopped their play as the man walked by.

"Why doesn't he answer when we call to him?" one of the boys asked.

The others shook their heads. They did not know. But they watched the man as he went on down the street alone.

A bird sang from a tree nearby. But the man did not look up; he did not stop to listen.

Once he tried to speak to a friend. But the friend just shook his head as if to say, "I cannot understand what you are trying to say."

Then someone shouted, "Jesus is coming!"

What wonderful news! The people in the little town were so glad that they ran to meet Jesus. All but the man. He just stood in the street and watched. Then two men turned back. They took the man by the hand and hurried him along. When they reached Jesus the men said, "Our friend cannot hear or speak. Please make him well."

Jesus looked at the man, and the man looked back. "He cares about me," the man thought to himself.

Jesus took the man away from the crowd. He put His fingers into the man's ears. He touched the man's tongue. He prayed to God. "Be opened," Jesus said.

And that very second the man could hear! For the first time in his life he could hear the birds; he could hear the wind in the trees! How wonderful it was!

And he could speak! "Oh, thank You! Thank You," he cried out to Jesus. How wonderful it was to tell someone how he felt!

Jesus smiled. He was glad the man could hear and speak. The man was glad, too. He was glad Jesus loved him enough to make him well.

People were amazed at what happened. And word of how much Jesus loved people and how He was able to heal those who had something wrong with them spread throughout the whole area.

Story based on Mark 7:31-37.

❦

Pray: Thank You, Jesus, that You love everyone and care about whatever is wrong with them. Help me to tell others about You.

Illustration by Elias Sallman, 1944

The Feeding of the Five Thousand

One day Jesus and His disciples were very tired. Jesus said, "Let's go get some rest." So they got into a boat and sailed over to the other side of a large lake called the Sea of Galilee.

But the crowds of people heard where they were going and began walking around the end of the lake and met them.

Even though He was tired, Jesus cared for the people and healed their sick. Then He spent the afternoon telling them how much God loved them. He talked for a long time. When He stopped, He knew the people were hungry.

"We need some food for these people," Jesus told His disciples. "Where can we get it?"

They shook their heads. "We do not have any food with us. And it would take a lot of money to buy enough food for this crowd. There are over five thousand people here. We do not have that much money."

Just then a little boy ran up. He held a basket in his hands.

"I have some food," he said. "It isn't much, but you may have it."

Jesus' disciples smiled. They knew the boy's lunch would not feed very many people. But they turned to Jesus. "It has only five little loaves of bread and two fish," laughed Andrew. "That won't go very far."

But Jesus thanked the boy for his lunch. "Have the people sit down on the grass," said Jesus. Then He prayed and began to break the fish and the bread into pieces. "Give these to the people," said Jesus.

The disciples passed out the pieces of bread and fish. When they came back, they could hardly believe what they saw. Jesus was still breaking off pieces of the little lunch.

So the disciples kept passing it out until everyone had eaten. Then they picked up the leftovers.

"Look!" said one of the disciples. "There are twelve baskets of bread and fish left over."

"Only Jesus could do such a wonderful thing," said another disciple.

The people wanted to crown Jesus king right then, but Jesus knew that they did not really understand who He was and why He had come into the world, so He withdrew to a mountain to pray by Himself.

Story based on John 6:1-15.

❦

Something to Think About: How would you have felt if you would have been the boy who offered his lunch to Jesus? What could you offer to Him?

Illustration by Fred Schnaple, 1937

114

Jesus Walks on Water

*I*n the evening after Jesus had fed the five thousand people on the hillside by the great lake, He sent them home. Then He told the disciples to get back into their boat and go back to the other side of the lake, too, while He went up onto the mountain to pray.

As night came on, the wind began to blow while the disciples were trying to make their boat go right into the wind. So they had to let down their sail and row the boat.

Time passed as the wind blew harder and the waves got bigger. The disciples were not making much headway rowing against the storm. It looked like it was going to be a long, miserable night. Some even began to worry that the boat might sink and they all would be drowned.

Then suddenly Andrew pointed across the lake. "Look!" he cried. "Something is coming across the water!"

"It looks like a man," said Peter, "but men can't walk on the water. What can it be?"

Everyone in the boat was afraid.

Then a Voice spoke. "Don't be afraid. It is I."

"It's Jesus!" said the disciples. "He is walking on the stormy sea."

"If it's really You," said Peter excitedly, "let me walk to You."

"Come," said Jesus.

Peter climbed out of the boat and began walking on the water toward Jesus.

Suddenly Peter stopped. He looked at the wind, and he looked down at the waves. "I can't really walk on water," he thought. Then Peter became afraid and began to sink.

"Help," he called to Jesus. "Save me!"

Immediately Jesus reached out and lifted Peter up on the water again.

"Why did you stop believing that I would help you?" He asked.

When they climbed into the boat the storm ended.

"We know now that You are God's Son," the disciples said. "No one else could do what You have done."

Story based on Matthew 14:22-33.

❧

Something to Think About: Why do you think Peter began to sink when he noticed the wind and the waves?

Illustration by Richard Hook

116

The Good Samaritan

Jesus told many stories to people. He liked to teach with stories that they could easily understand.

One day a teacher of the law asked Jesus, "What must I do to please God and go to heaven?"

"You're a teacher," Jesus said. "What does the law say?"

"Well," said the man, "It says, 'Love the Lord your God with all your heart and your neighbor as yourself.'"

"That's the right answer," said Jesus. "Do that, and you will live."

But the man was trying to make himself look smart in the eyes of the other people, so he asked a question he thought Jesus couldn't answer: "Yes, but who is my neighbor?"

In response Jesus told this story to show how to be a good friend and neighbor:

Once a man was walking on a road. Suddenly some robbers jumped on him. They beat the man. They took his money. They left him lying by the road.

The man was hurt very badly. He had cuts on him. He could not get up and walk to the city. "I need someone to help me," he cried.

Then he saw someone coming. It was a temple priest. "He will help me," thought the man.

But the priest was not a good person. He did not want to help the man. So he walked past him.

The sick man lay for a long time. At last someone else came along the road. "It's a priest's helper," said the sick man. "Surely he will take care of me." But the priest's helper would not stop either.

The sick man lay very still. At last another man came down the road. "This man will not help me," said the sick man. "He lives in Samaria. People there do not like people in my country."

But the man from Samaria did stop. He helped the sick man. He took him to an inn so he could rest.

"Take care of this hurt man," said the man from Samaria to the innkeeper. "I will pay for your help."

When Jesus finished the story He asked the teacher of the law, "Which man was a good friend and neighbor?"

"The man from Samaria," he answered.

"Then be a good friend and neighbor like the man from Samaria," said Jesus.

Story based on Luke 10:25-37.

❧

Something to Think About: Why do you think the priest and the priest's helper did not help the hurt man? Who might you be friends to that other people might ignore?

Illustration by Fred Schnaple, 1936

118

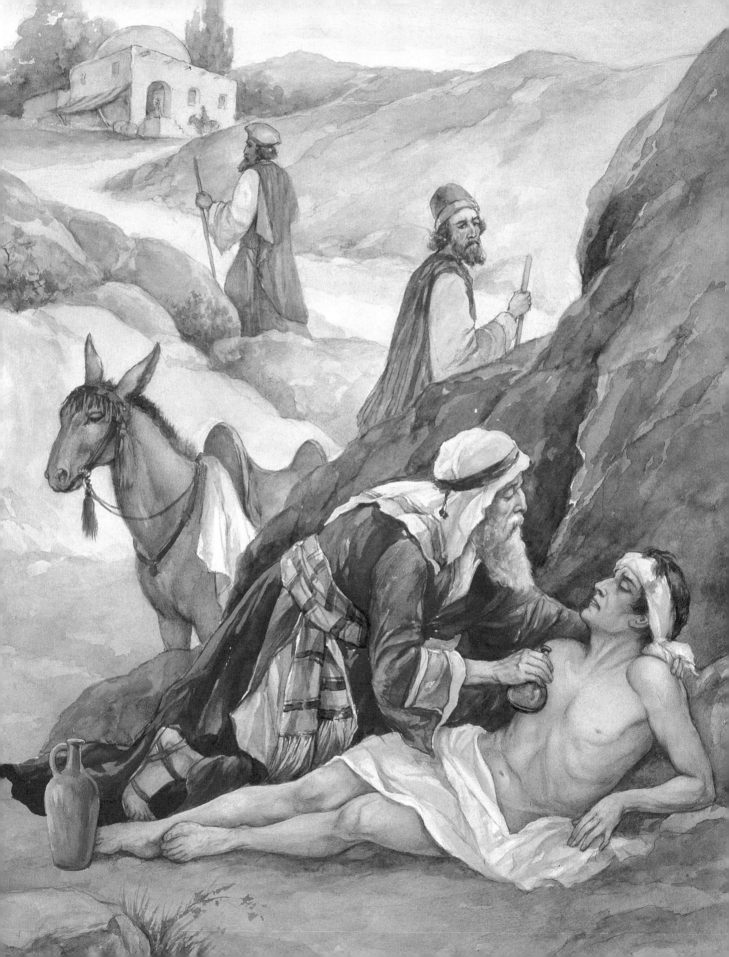

Jesus' Friends in Bethany

Jesus enjoyed visiting His good friends, Mary and Martha and their brother Lazarus. They lived in a nice home in Bethany, a small town near Jerusalem. And they were always happy to have Jesus as their guest.

One day they heard that Jesus was coming to their house. They hoped He would stay, have supper, and rest for a while.

When Jesus got there, He did agree to stay for a while. Martha was so happy that she hurried into the kitchen and began to prepare a big feast. "I will bake fresh bread and cakes, and roast a leg of lamb," she told herself.

But Mary stayed with Jesus. She wanted to hear Him tell about God and how God wanted people to live their lives.

At last Martha came into the room where Jesus and Mary were sitting. Her face was hot and red, and she looked cross.

"Jesus," she asked, "do You think it is fair for me to be doing all the work while Mary sits in here doing nothing? Tell her to help me."

Jesus shook His head sadly. He knew Martha loved Him and wanted to be kind to Him. And He knew that the work had to get done.

Illustration by Elias Sallman, 1946

But in His kindly way Jesus said, "Martha, you are making yourself tired doing a lot of things. But being with Me and learning about God is more important. That is what Mary has chosen to do. Why don't you come and join us?"

Story based on Luke 10:38-42.

❧

Something to Think About: Why is being with Jesus and listening to what He has to say more important than doing a lot of good works for Jesus? How can you listen to Jesus?

120

Jesus Loves the Children

The children were so happy. They had wanted to see Jesus for so long. Now Jesus was coming. Now they would see Him. They sang and clapped their hands as they came to the place where Jesus was. But there was a big crowd around Jesus. They couldn't see Him.

The mothers tried to help their children push through the crowd. At last they came near Jesus.

Then some men stepped in the way. They were Jesus' helpers. "Can't you see that Jesus is busy?" they asked. "Jesus doesn't have time to see little children."

The little children were so sad. They wanted to see Jesus, even if He was busy.

"Let the children come to Me," Someone said. Everyone looked to see who had said that. It was Jesus.

The children ran to Jesus. They were so happy now.

Jesus brought the children around Him. He began to tell them wonderful things about God.

"God loves you very much" He told the children. "And I love you, too."

Then Jesus turned to the crowd and said, "It is important to help the children come to me. The kingdom of God belongs to people like them. This is because they have the kind of trust and faith that pleases God."

And then Jesus gave the people a very strong warning that showed how much He loved and cared for children. He said, "If anyone causes one of these little ones to sin, it would be better for him if a great stone were hung around his neck and he was thrown into the sea to drown."

And then Jesus took the children in His arms and blessed them.

On the way home a happy boy walked with his mother. "I'm glad God loves me," he said.

The mother smiled. "How do you know?" she asked.

"Because He sent Jesus to be my special Friend," the boy answered.

Story based on Matthew 18:6 and Mark 10:13-16.

❦

Something to Think About: What did Jesus mean when He said that the children had the kind of faith and trust that pleased God?

Illustration by Richard Hook

122

The Prodigal Son

Jesus told many stories. Once He told a story about a father and his son.

The father had two sons. He loved them very much. But one day the younger son said, "Give me the money that will be mine someday. I want to leave home and do as I please."

The father did not like to see his son leave home because he did not think his son was ready to live in a good way. But he gave him the money anyway.

The son went far away from his home. He spent his money on fine clothes and wild parties. But one day he found that his money was all gone.

When his money was gone, his friends left him, too. He had no one to help him. He had nothing to eat.

The foolish son went out to get a job. He took care of a farmer's pigs. He was very, very poor. He was so poor and hungry that he wanted to eat the pigs' food.

Finally, the foolish son began to think. "My father's servants have more than I do. I will go home and apologize to my father for being so foolish. Then I will ask my father if I can at least work for him."

As he came near his home, the foolish son was afraid. He wondered if his father would be angry with him. Perhaps he would not even let him be a servant. What should he say to his father?

Illustration by R. Holberg, 1941

124

Then the foolish son saw his father running down the road. His father threw his arms around him. "How glad I am to see you again," the father cried.

The father was so joyful that his son had returned that he gave a feast for his foolish son. He wanted to show how much he loved him. He wanted to show that he was not angry with his son who had done so many wrong things. He was a *prodigal* son. That means that even though he had done wrong, he had repented of his wrong and had come home.

The people knew what Jesus was saying. They knew that God forgives us when we ask Him, just as the father forgave his son.

Story based on Luke 15:1, 11-32.

❧

Pray: Jesus, please help me remember that whenever I do something wrong, You are ready and eager to forgive me and welcome me back to be close to You.

Two Men Who Went to Pray

Jesus was talking to a crowd of people, but some of them were standing off by themselves. They thought they were too good to be with the others.

So Jesus told them a story about two men. One man in His story was a Pharisee. A Pharisee was a man who was very strict about keeping religious rules. And the other man was a tax collector. Nobody liked tax collectors because they got rich by taking too much money and they helped the Roman government that ruled their land. They were almost like traitors.

The two men went to God's house to pray. The Pharisee prayed in a loud voice so that all the people could hear. "O God," he said, "I thank You that I am not like people who are greedy and selfish—or like that tax collector. I keep your rules and I give part of what I have to You."

The tax collector stood back in the corner by himself. He bowed his head and spoke in a voice so low that only God could hear. "O God," he prayed, "I know that I have sinned. Forgive me for all the wrong things I have done."

Then Jesus turned to the people and told them that the tax collector went home a happy man because God had forgiven him and that made him right with God.

Illustration by Richard Hook

"The other man did not impress God," said Jesus. "Anyone who thinks he is better than others is not great in God's eyes. But the man who is honest with God will be great."

You see, the Pharisee was not really praying to God. He was telling people how great he was. The tax collector, on the other hand, was really talking to God; he knew he had done wrong and he wanted God to forgive him.

Story based on Luke 18:9-14.

❧

Something to Think About: What are some ways people today try to appear very religious even when their hearts might not be right with God?

126

The Blind Man by the Road

Every day a man sat by the side of the road. He couldn't see people pass by. The man was blind. But he could hear people laugh and talk. When he heard them he held out his hand. "I'm hungry! Give me some money to buy food," he begged.

One day the man heard many people. They were coming down the road.

"What is going on?" he asked. "Please tell me."

"Jesus is going to Jericho. Many people are going along to hear what He says," a man said.

The blind man didn't wait to hear more. "Oh, Jesus," he yelled out. "Help me! Help me!"

"Be quiet," a man said in a rough voice. But the blind man would not be quiet.

"Jesus, help me," he cried.

Jesus stopped. "Bring the man to Me," He said.

Some men in the crowd brought the man to Jesus.

"What do you want Me to do?" Jesus asked.

"Oh, Lord," the man said, "help me to see."

"Receive your sight," said Jesus. "You can now see because you believed that I could help you."

The man opened his eyes. "I can see!" he cried. He looked at Jesus. At the blue sky—the sunlight on the hills. Oh, how wonderful it was to see!

He looked at Jesus again. "Praise God for sending You to help me," he said.

The people with Jesus were surprised. They could hardly believe their own eyes. But they were happy for the man who could see. And they praised God for sending Jesus.

Story based on Luke 18:35-43.

❧

Pray: Dear Lord, thank You for coming to earth to help the blind man. Help me to trust You like he did.

Illustration by Fred Schnaple, 1936

The Little Man in a Tree

Zacchaeus was a very rich man. But nobody liked Zacchaeus because he was a tax collector. "He takes money from us," they said. "He gives some of it to the Romans who rule over us. And he keeps some for himself."

"He cheats," others said.

One day Zacchaeus heard people shouting in the street. "What is happening?" he asked.

"Jesus is here!" they said.

Zacchaeus wanted to see Jesus, too. But he was a very short man. He was too little to see over the other people.

Then Zacchaeus had an idea. He ran down the road until he came to a big tree. He climbed up into the tree and sat on one of the big branches. Now he would be able to see Jesus.

Zacchaeus saw the crowd coming closer to the tree. Then he saw Jesus. "How tall and strong He looks," Zacchaeus thought. "I know He would never cheat people like I do." Then Zacchaeus began to wish he could talk to Jesus.

When Jesus came under the tree, He stopped. Then He looked up at Zacchaeus.

"Zacchaeus," said Jesus. "Come down. I want to go to your house today."

Zacchaeus was so happy. He could hardly believe what Jesus had said. He jumped down from the tree and ran to Jesus.

But the people who were with Jesus began to mutter and said, "Why is Jesus going to a sinner's house?"

Then Zacchaeus felt sad because of all the cheating he had done. He looked at Jesus. "I'm sorry for what I have done," he said. "Here and now I give half of my possessions to the poor. And if I have cheated anyone, I'll pay back four times what I took."

"Your repentance pleases God," said Jesus. "This is the very reason God sent Me—to find people like you so I can help them."

Story based on Luke 19:1-10.

❦

Something to Think About: Why did the people dislike Zacchaeus? What made God pleased with Zacchaeus? How can we please God?

Illustration by Milo Winter 1938

The Widow's Offering

One day Jesus went to the courtyard of the temple where He often taught the people.

As he stood to one side, a rich man walked into God's house. He stopped and looked around. He waited until everyone in the temple saw him. Then he went to the place where people gave their gifts to God. Slowly he dropped many coins into the box. He seemed to say, "See how much money I am giving to God."

The mothers and fathers and children looked around. Jesus had seen what had happened. "I wonder what Jesus thinks of the rich man's gift?" they said to each other. But Jesus looked sad. He seemed sorry for the man who had acted so proud of the money he had given to God.

Soon after that a poor woman came in. Her clothes were old. Quietly she went to the box. She dropped in two little coins. Then she hurried away.

The mothers and fathers and children looked at Jesus. There was a smile on His face.

"Look!" the children whispered. "The woman gave just two little coins, but Jesus is pleased."

Then the children listened. Jesus was talking to some of His disciples.

"The poor woman gave the best gift of all," Jesus said to His friends. "The rich man gave only a little part of what he has. The poor woman gave everything she had."

"She must love God very much," the children said to their mothers and fathers.

"Yes," said one of the fathers. "That is why Jesus is pleased. You see, the rich man loves himself. The poor woman loves God."

Story based on Mark 12:41-44.

❦

Something to Think About: Why wouldn't God want more money and be happy with all the money the rich man could give? Does God need our money? Why do we give offerings?

Illustration by Fred Schnaple, 1936

132

A New Life for Lazarus

One day Lazarus, the brother of Mary and Martha, Jesus' good friends in Bethany, got very sick. No one could help him. "What if Lazarus dies?" thought the sisters. "Please go find Jesus," they asked a friend. "Tell Him Lazarus is very sick."

Mary and Martha and Lazarus waited and waited. But Jesus did not come. At last Lazarus died.

The two sisters cried and cried. They buried Lazarus in a cave. "If only Jesus had come," they said. "He could have healed Lazarus."

Four days later Jesus finally arrived. Martha ran to meet Him. She began to cry. "Lazarus is dead," she said. "If only You had come before. You could have healed him."

"God can do wonderful things," said Jesus. "You will see now what God can do. Take Me to the place where you buried Lazarus."

So Mary and Martha and Jesus went to the cave where Lazarus was buried.

Jesus stood near the cave. "Lazarus," He called, "come out of the cave!"

Mary and Martha looked at each other. What was Jesus saying? How could Lazarus come out when he was dead?

But Lazarus did come out. He was alive again.

The two sisters were happy to have Lazarus with them again. "God can do wonderful things," they said. "He can even bring dead people back to life again."

Many of the Jews who had come to comfort Mary and Martha when Lazarus died were there when Jesus raised him from the dead. And many of them believed on Jesus.

But when some of the religious leaders in Jerusalem heard about the event, they feared that everyone would believe in Jesus and not follow them. So they planned to kill Him when he came to Jerusalem to celebrate the Passover feast.

Story based on John 11:1-44.

❧

Pray: Dear Lord, please help me to be patient if You don't do what I ask right when I ask it. Please help me to trust that You have the power to do anything and make what seems terrible finally turn out for good.

Illustration by Fred Schnaple, 1937

134

Jesus Welcomed in Jerusalem

The next day Jesus and His disciples traveled on toward Jerusalem. And sent two of His disciples on ahead. "You will find a donkey and her colt tied there. Untie them, and bring them to Me."

"What if someone asks us what we are doing?" one of the disciples asked.

"Just tell him that the Lord needs them," answered Jesus.

So the disciples went ahead and did as Jesus instructed them. And just as they were leaving a man came running out of his house.

"Stop!" he shouted. "Why are you taking my donkey?"

"Uh-oh," said one of the disciples. "Now we're in trouble."

"Maybe not," said the other. "Remember what Jesus said?"

"Jesus wants to use your donkey," they called out to the man.

The man smiled. "If Jesus wants to use it, please take it," he said. "No. Wait a minute," and he ran back in his house. A moment later he came out with a beautiful blanket. "Here," he said. "Put this on the donkey's back for Jesus to ride upon."

"Jesus never makes a mistake, does He?" said the disciples as they walked back to Jesus.

Jesus climbed onto the donkey's back. He began riding toward Jerusalem.

When people saw Jesus riding on the donkey, they ran along the road.

"Jesus is coming!" they shouted.

Some people threw their coats on the road for Jesus to ride on. Others cut palm branches from trees and threw them on the road.

The people shouted and sang. "Blessed is Jesus, for He comes in the name of the Lord," they said.

"Jesus looks like a king," a boy whispered.

"Jesus is a King," his father answered. "He is a good King who does not make war. He does not make us work for Him. He tells us about God."

When Jesus rode into Jerusalem, people ran to see Him. They brought sick people for Him to heal. They brought blind people so He could make them see.

"Praise be to God," the people shouted. "We will always remember this day."

But the Pharisees and the Jewish leaders were not happy. "Look," they said, "the whole world is following Him. This is getting out of hand. We must do something soon."

Story based on John 12:12-19 and Matthew 21:1-16.

❧

Something to Think About: Why do you think the man was happy to let Jesus use his donkey? Why do you think the Jewish leaders were unhappy?

Illustration by Hockings, 1940

136

Jesus Is Arrested

*J*esus knew that the excitement of the people who had welcomed Him so joyfully when He rode into Jerusalem would make the Jewish leaders angry and afraid. They were angry because they didn't want to repent of their sin and accept Jesus as their king. And they were afraid that the Romans would think Jesus was starting a revolt.

Before the week was out, these leaders made a plan to arrest Jesus. They paid Judas thirty pieces of silver to become a traitor and help them catch Him. Judas was the disciple whose heart wasn't right with God.

After eating the Passover meal with His disciples, Jesus told them what was going to happen—that He would be arrested and put to death.

And sure enough, later that night when they were out in the Garden of Gethsemane, Judas led the Jewish leaders armed with swords and clubs to where Jesus was praying. To show the Jewish leaders who to arrest, Judas kissed Jesus.

Then they arrested Jesus.

At first, Peter tried to be brave, ready to fight. He even swung his sword and cut off the right ear of the high priest's servant. But Jesus said, "Put away your sword. Everyone who uses violence will die by violence." Then Jesus touched the ear and healed it. "Besides," said Jesus, "if I wanted protection, I could pray and God would send thousands and thousands of angels to defend Me. But we must let this happen just the way the Old Testament prophecies said it would happen."

But soon all the disciples became so afraid that they ran away and left Jesus alone with His captors.

Jesus' trial lasted all night. First He was taken before Caiaphas, the high priest. Then Jesus was tried by Pilate, the Roman governor. But Pilate could not find any reason to condemn Him because Jesus hadn't done anything wrong. Pilate sent Him to Herod, another Roman ruler, but he couldn't find anything wrong with Jesus, so he sent Jesus back to Pilate.

Finally, to please the Jewish leaders, Pilate had Jesus cruelly whipped and the soldiers put a crown of thorns on His head and a royal-looking robe on Him to make fun of Him. But still the crowd yelled, "Kill Him. Hang Him on a cross till He dies." So Pilate gave in and approved the crucifixion of Jesus.

*Story based on Matthew 26, 27;
Luke 23; John 18, 19.*

❧

Something to Think About: Why didn't Jesus want to fight those who came to arrest Him? Why do you think the disciples became afraid and ran away?

*Illustration by
Fred Schnaple,
1937*

138

The Crucifixion of Jesus Christ

After Jesus was condemned, the soldiers took Him out of the city to a hill called the Skull. They fastened Jesus to the cross by putting nails through His hands and feet and then standing the cross up so that Jesus hung above the crowd.

And just like the prophet Isaiah had predicted in the Old Testament, Jesus was treated like an ordinary criminal. In fact, two robbers were crucified with Him, one on each side.

However, Pilate put a sign above Jesus' head to tell everyone why He was being crucified. Of course, Pilate had not found anything wrong with Jesus, so he wrote the truth: "This is Jesus, the King of the Jews."

This upset the Jewish leaders because the Old Testament had prophesied that God would send a Messiah who would be their King. How awful it would sound if they had rejected and killed Him. So they asked Pilate to change the sign to say: "He *said* that He was the King of the Jews." But Pilate would not change it.

While Jesus was suffering on the cross, the soldiers divided His clothes. "Let's not tear this valuable garment," they said. "It's all one piece, without any seams." So they decided who would get it by rolling dice. Hundreds of years earlier in the Old Testament, this is exactly what David had predicted would happen, and God was causing it to come true.

At noon, a strange darkness fell across the land just as the prophet

Illustration by Fred Schnaple, 1936

140

Amos prophesied. It lasted until three o'clock in the afternoon when Jesus cried out to God and said, "Father, into Your hands I place My spirit." Then He died. Suddenly there was a tremendous earthquake.

Seeing these strange things, the commander and other soldiers were terrified, and said, "Certainly He was the Son of God." Many other people were also afraid and were convinced that a very terrible thing had happened that day.

A rich man named Joseph from Arimathea asked Pilate for Jesus' body in order to bury it in his own tomb. Pilate granted his request. And a huge stone was rolled across the tomb's door.

Remembering how Jesus had said He would rise from the dead, the Jewish leaders had Pilate post Roman soldiers to guard the tomb and prevent anyone from disturbing the body.

Story based on Matthew 27, Luke 23, and John 19.

❧

Something to Think About: Why do you think Jesus willingly allowed Himself to be crucified? What do all the fulfilled prophecies show about Jesus?

Back from the Grave

It was early Sunday morning. The sky was dark and the city of Jerusalem was still. Three women hurried down the street. They were going to the tomb where Jesus was buried.

"The whole world seems as sad as we are," Mary Magdalene said to her friends, the mother of James and Salome.

Mary was sad, but she was angry, too. "How could those wicked men put Jesus to death?" she asked.

"They were afraid people would obey Jesus instead of them," the mother of James answered. Then, suddenly, she stopped for a minute. "Who will roll the stone away from Jesus' tomb?" she asked.

"If we can't get into the tomb, how can we put our spices on Jesus' body?" asked Salome.

But the women did not have to worry, for when they came to the tomb it was already open! And an angel sat on the big stone beside it. It was like looking at a bright light, for the angel's face shone and his robes were glistening white like snow.

The usually brave Roman guards were so frightened of the angel that they shook and became like dead men.

"Do not be afraid," the angel said to the women. "Jesus is not here. He has risen from the dead, just as He said. Go, tell the disciples that Jesus has risen from the dead."

The women were still afraid, but they were excited, too. They turned and ran back the way they had come.

And on the way they met Jesus. He greeted them in His kindly way, and they fell down and worshiped Him.

Then Jesus said, "Go, tell My friends that I will meet them in Galilee."

Now it was the brightest, happiest day in all the world!

"What wonderful news we have to tell," the women cried. "Jesus is alive!"

While the women went to find the disciples, the guards recovered enough from their terror to go tell the Jewish leaders everything that had happened. They paid the soldiers a large sum of money to tell a lie that the disciples stole Jesus' body.

"But we may be put to death if our commander hears that story," they objected. "It makes it look like we weren't doing our job while we were on guard duty."

"Don't worry," said the leaders. "We'll work things out with the governor."

So the soldiers took the money and told the lie.

Story based on Matthew 28:1-10 and Mark 16:1-8.

❧

Pray: Lord, thank You for being willing to die on the cross for my sins. But thank You even more for being God and for coming back to life.

Illustration by Joe Tillotson, 1949

142

Breakfast by the Sea

The disciples were afraid of the Jewish leaders, so they stayed hidden as much as possible and only met together in a private room. Twice Jesus came to be with them. Both times He suddenly appeared among them even though the door was locked and there was no other way for Him to get into the room.

He showed them his wounds and encouraged them to touch Him to prove He wasn't a ghost. Then He encouraged them to carry on His ministry, to go out among the people and share the Good News that He had risen from the dead and is the Son of God.

Later, several of the disciples were together by the Sea of Galilee when Peter said. "I think I'll go fishing."

"I'll go with you," John said.

"And so will I," said another—and then another. Soon seven men were in the boat.

They fished all night, but they didn't catch any fish. At daylight they turned their boat back toward land.

"Have you caught anything?" a Voice called out.

Peter and the others looked. They saw a Man standing on the shore. "No," they shouted back.

"Throw your net over the right side of the boat," the Man called.

At first the fishermen thought, what is the use? But there was something about the voice that made them obey. Almost at once the net was full of fish.

John looked toward the Man on the shore. "Peter!" John cried. "It's the Lord! This is just like the first time He called us to become fishers of men. Remember? Our boats almost sank; we caught so many fish when we did what He told us to do."

"You're right," said Peter. He was so excited that he jumped into the water and swam to shore. The others brought the boat in—dragging the net of fish behind them.

"Look," one of the fishermen said. "Jesus has built a fire and cooked breakfast."

"Isn't it just like Jesus to do something for us?" another one of the men asked.

When they had finished eating, Jesus said to Peter, "Take care of My friends."

Then Jesus left them. But the men were not sad. Jesus promised to see them again. And Jesus always kept His promise.

Story based on John 20:19—21:17.

❧

Pray: Jesus, help me to believe more completely that You are God's Son, that You did rise from the dead, and that You are my Savior-King.

Illustration by Fred Schnaple, 1935

144

Jesus Goes Back to Heaven

Jesus is alive!" His disciples told the wonderful news to all His friends in in the country by the Sea of Galilee.

"Alive?" the friends asked in surprise. "How can that be? Jesus was put to death on a cross. How can a man who was dead come to life?"

"Jesus is not a man like any of us," the disciples said. "He is God's Son, and God brought Him back to life. We know it—we have seen Him."

The wonderful news spread. Soon people were shouting. "We're going to see Jesus!"

A large crowd of over five hundred people gathered on a hillside covered with grass and flowers. And Jesus came to them and spoke to them so that every one could be sure it was really Him.

"I want you to teach the people everywhere all the things I have taught you," Jesus said.

How happy the people were. They listened and promised to obey.

One day when they had returned to Jerusalem, Jesus took His disciples to a place called the Mount of Olives. It had been forty days since He rose from the dead.

At the top of the mountain Jesus blessed them and told them to wait in Jerusalem until He sent His Holy Spirit to them. The Holy Spirit would give them the power they would need to preach the Gospel in Jerusalem and in all the world.

And while Jesus was blessing them, a strange thing happened. He was taken up into the sky. The men watched. A cloud covered Jesus. He was gone from their sight. Jesus had returned to heaven to be with God, His Father!

And as they were looking up into the sky, suddenly two angels stood beside them and said, "Men of Galilee, why are you looking up into the sky? This same Jesus who has been taken up into heaven will come back again in the same way you have seen Him go."

So the disciples went back into the city. They were not afraid. They knew Jesus would always be near them. And someday they would be with Him again.

Story based on Acts 1:1-12;
I Corinthians 15:6.

❧

Something to Think About: Why do you think Jesus stayed on earth for forty days after He rose from the dead before He returned to heaven?

Illustration by Fred Schnaple, 1936

146

The Holy Spirit and the Church

Ten days after Jesus went back to heaven, all of His followers were together, waiting for the Holy Spirit whom Jesus had promised to send. They knew that they would need His power to began preaching to those who didn't believe.

Suddenly, while they were praying and singing and praising God, there was a sound like a mighty wind. What seemed like little flames of fire appeared above everyone. And everyone was filled with the Holy Spirit and began to speak in different languages so that every foreigner who heard them, heard his or her own language being spoken.

Then Peter began to preach about Jesus, and about three thousand people believed and were baptized that day.

It was a tremendous start to the new church, and the people listened carefully to how the disciples said they should live together and love each other.

For instance, one young boy watched as his mother packed some bread and cheese and figs into a big basket. When she finished his father counted out some coins. "This is the money I got from selling my sheep yesterday," he said.

The mother nodded. "There are people who need the money more than we do."

"But what can I give?" asked the boy. He, too, had heard the disciples teach how Jesus wanted His followers to love and share with one another.

The mother and father were surprised. "Why—" they started to say. Then they smiled. "Of course. Decide what you would like to give."

"I will give my other pair of sandals. They are almost new," he said.

So the mother and father and boy walked through the streets of Jerusalem until they reached a house where Peter and some of Jesus' followers were gathered. Peter took the food and the money and the sandals.

After he thanked God for them, he gave the coins to some men who looked as if they needed them. He gave the sandals to a boy who was barefoot. Then he put the food with some that other women had brought. Finally, they all sat down and ate together.

And as they ate Peter talked about Jesus. "Jesus wants His friends to work together and to share what they have with each other," Peter said.

The boy smiled. It felt good to be a friend of Jesus.

Story based on Acts 2.

❦

Something to Think About: What are some ways you could express your love for others by sharing?

Illustration by Joe Tillotson, 1950

148

Peter and John Heal the Cripple

Peter and John were going to the temple to pray. They saw a man sitting by the gate. The man stopped them.

"I cannot walk," the man said. "Please give me some money to buy food."

Peter and John looked at the man. He was not old. But he looked old. He looked sad, too.

"I have no money," Peter said. "But I will do what I can for you. In Jesus' name, stand up and walk."

Peter took the man by the hand. The man stood up—for the first time in his whole life. Instantly his feet and ankles became strong. He started running and jumping into the temple courts.

"Praise God," he cried. "I can walk!"

The people were surprised. They looked at the man and recognized that he was the man who used to sit begging at the temple gate.

Then they looked at Peter. "I did not make the man walk by my own power or goodness," Peter said. "God did it. He loves His Son, Jesus. He wants us to love Him, too."

When Jesus' enemies heard what Peter said, they were angry. They did not believe that Jesus was God's Son. They did not want anyone else to believe it either.

"Arrest Peter and John," Jesus' enemies said. So Peter and John were arrested.

"We will let you go this time," Jesus' enemies said. "But you must never speak about Jesus again. We will punish you if you do."

Jesus' enemies thought they could scare Peter and John. But they couldn't.

"We will never stop talking about Jesus," Peter and John said bravely. And they went back out into the streets preaching about Jesus and healing many.

Again, the Jewish leaders arrested them and put them in jail. But during the night an angel opened the doors of the jail and released them.

The next day, the disciples were again preaching.

The Jewish leaders brought them in for questioning. "We gave you strict orders to never speak about Jesus again. Why aren't you obeying us?"

The Peter answered, "We must obey God rather than men!"

And they did, no matter what happened.

Story based on Acts 3—5.

❧

Something to Think About: Why did Peter and John say that they must obey God rather than men? What had God told them to do?

Illustration by Fred Schnaple, 1936

150

Philip and the Ethiopian

Philip had been chosen by the believers in Jerusalem to help minister to the church. The Holy Spirit filled him with power, and he went to a city in Samaria to preach the Gospel.

Many people believed and were healed.

Then one day an angel of the Lord said to Philip, "I want you to go south to the road that leads from Jerusalem to Gaza."

Now this was the long desert road that people traveled when they were going to and from Africa. And as Philip walked along, he met an important African official from the country of Ethiopia.

This man had gone to Jerusalem to worship God and was on his way home. He was riding in his chariot, reading the Book of Isaiah the prophet.

"Do you understand what you are reading?" Philip called to him.

"How can I," answered the African, "unless someone explains it to me?"

So he invited Philip to ride with him and explain the Scriptures.

It so happened that the African was reading some of Isaiah's prophecies about the coming of the Messiah, the Savior-King. "Tell me," said the African, "who was this prophet talking about?"

Illustration by
Joe Tillotson

So Philip started with those very verses and told him about Jesus Christ and how God's Savior-King had just come.

"This is great news," said the African. "How happy I am to hear it. How can I express my desire to follow Jesus?"

Philip explained, and as they were traveling along the road, they came to some water and the African said, "Well, I believe and want to give my life to Jesus, and there is some water. Why shouldn't I be baptized right now?"

So they stopped the chariot, and he and Philip went down into the water and Philip baptized him.

When they came up out of the water, the Spirit of the Lord suddenly took Philip away, and the African did not see him again. But he was so happy at hearing the Gospel that he went on his way singing and praising God.

And it is believed by many Africans that this important official was the first one to bring Christianity to their country.

As for Philip, the Spirit of the Lord caused him to appear in a city many miles away. There Philip continued to preach about Jesus as he traveled on back north to Samaria.

Story based on Acts 8:26-40.

❧

Pray: Lord, please help me be ready to speak to others about the Good News that You came to be our Savior-King.

152

Paul's Conversion

Paul was in a hurry. He was going to Damascus to arrest some followers of Jesus. Paul did not believe Jesus was God's Son. Paul worked for the Jewish leaders that wanted to stop people from following Jesus. He thought God wanted him to arrest people who believed in Jesus.

Paul rode on and on. Suddenly a light shone around him. It was brighter than the sun. Paul fell down on the ground. A Voice spoke to him. "Why are you being so cruel to Me?"

Paul was so surprised he could hardly speak. "Who are you?" he asked.

"I am Jesus, the One you are treating so badly," the voice said.

Jesus was dead, Paul thought. But He is talking to me! God must have made this happen.

"What do You want me to do?" Paul asked.

"Go into the city," Jesus said. "You will be told what to do."

Paul stood up, but he could not see. His friends had to lead him into the city. They took him to the house of a man named Judas. Paul waited and prayed.

In that same city there lived a follower of Jesus named Ananias. The Lord spoke to him in a vision and said, "I want you to go to the house of Judas and ask for a man named Paul. He is waiting for you."

"I've heard about this Paul," said Ananias. "He has already done much harm to Your church, and he's coming here to do more."

But the Lord said, "Go anyway. Paul is ready to repent, and I want him for My servant."

So Ananias went to Paul and put his hands on him. "Jesus sent me to help you," Ananias said.

Immediately Paul could see again. He was happy. "I believe that Jesus is God's Son," he said. "I believe God raised Him from the dead."

So Paul found the best way of all to please God. He was baptized and began teaching people about Jesus.

Story based on Acts 9:1-20.

❧

Something to Think About: Why was Paul wanting to arrest those who believed in Jesus? Why did he change? How can we please God?

Illustration by Fred Schnaple, 1936

154

The Gate That Opened by Itself

A wicked king did not want Peter to teach people about Jesus. But Peter would not stop. So the king had Peter put in prison again. Peter's right hand was chained to a soldier. His left hand was chained to another soldier. Two more soldiers stood at the door.

"Peter will never get away from us this time," the soldiers said. They pointed to their heavy swords.

One day the wicked king said, "I will have Peter killed tomorrow."

That night an angel came to Peter. "Get up," the angel said.

Peter got up. The chains fell off his hands. The soldiers did not move. They were like wooden soldiers. There wasn't a sound anyplace.

"Put on your coat and sandals and follow me," the angel said. Peter did. The angel led Peter through the prison. They passed the first and second guards. The angel led him to the big iron gate. It opened all by itself. They walked out into the street. Then the angel went away.

Peter ran down the street as fast as he could. He ran to the house of a woman called Mary where many of the believers were gathered praying for him.

He knocked on the outer entrance, and a girl named Rhoda came to the door. "Who is there?" she asked.

"It is I," Peter said in a low voice.

The girl was so excited that she did not even think to open the door. Instead she went back into the house.

"It's Peter!" she told the people. The people were Peter's friends. They shook their heads. "Oh, Rhoda," they said, "you must be mistaken. You are excited. You just think it is Peter."

"But it *is* Peter," Rhoda said. There was another knock on the big, wooden door.

Mary went. She opened the door. "Peter," she cried, "it *is* you! Come in! We have been praying for you."

"And God answered your prayers," Peter said. Then he told them how God's angel had brought him out of prison. "I want you to go tell James and the other disciples."

Then Peter went away before the soldiers found him again. But he kept right on teaching about Jesus—just as Jesus had asked him to do.

Story based on Acts 12:1-17.

❧

Something to Think About: What were the believers doing that helped Peter get out of prison? What can we do to help God's work succeed?

Illustration by Fred Schnaple, 1935

156

Paul and Silas Sing in Jail

Paul and Silas were in trouble. They had helped a slave girl by casting out an evil spirit from her. The wicked men who owned her were angry. They did not care about what was good for the girl, but they made money from her because they made her use the evil spirit to predict the future.

Now they couldn't make money, so they had Paul and Silas beaten and put in jail.

"Don't let Paul and Silas get away," the soldiers told the keeper of the jail. "If you do, you will be killed."

The jailer was afraid. He took Paul and Silas to a room in the middle of the jail. He locked their feet in heavy blocks of wood called stocks.

It was dark and wet in the jail. Paul and Silas's bodies hurt from the beating. But they were not afraid. They knew God had not forgotten them. They began to sing praises to God.

"How can they sing in jail?" the other men in jail asked. But Paul and Silas kept on singing praises to God.

Suddenly there was a great rumble. The walls shook. Doors flew open. Chains fell off men's hands and feet.

The keeper thought Paul and Silas had run away. He was afraid. "I might as well kill myself!" he cried.

"Don't kill yourself!" Paul called out in a loud voice. "See, we are all here. We have not run away."

The keeper called for a torch. He looked around the room. What Paul said was true. The keeper was sure now that Paul and Silas were special men of God. He ran to them and fell down on his knees before them.

"What must I do to be saved?" he asked.

"Believe in Jesus," Paul said. The keeper was happy to learn about Jesus. He took care of Paul and Silas's hurt bodies. Then he and all his family were baptized. How happy they were to learn about Jesus who loved them so much that He died on the cross for them.

Soon Paul and Silas were set free. After that they went on helping more and more people learn about Jesus.

Story based on Acts 16:16-40.

❧

Something to Think About: What must we do to be saved? What does that mean?

Illustration by Fred Schnaple, 1936

158

The Ride in the Night

Paul went on three long missionary journeys. But when he returned to Jerusalem, there were some men there who did not like him because he said that Jesus was God's Son.

One day when Paul was teaching in the temple, these men came in and stirred up the crowd. To avoid a riot, the Roman captain arrested Paul and was going to have him whipped. Paul was in danger, but it was illegal to punish a Roman citizen without a trial. So Paul let the Roman captain know that he was a Roman citizen.

The captain could have been in big trouble if any harm had come to Paul before a fair trial, so he put Paul in prison until he could be tried.

"We must get rid of Paul," the Jewish leaders said. "If people believe what he tells them they will not listen to us."

One day one of these leaders said to some friends, "I have a plan. The Roman soldiers are holding Paul. We will ask the soldiers to bring Paul before our judges. But on the way we will have someone kill him."

"Good!" said another man. "Let us make a promise. We will not eat or drink until Paul is killed!"

"We promise!" the others shouted.

The men were excited. But they talked so much about their plan that a boy heard them. He was actually Paul's nephew. He bravely ran to the place where Paul was. "Uncle Paul," the boy whispered through the bars on the prison window. "Your enemies are going to kill you."

Paul called a soldier. "Take this boy to the captain," he said. The soldier obeyed Paul.

The boy told the Roman captain what he had heard. "Go home," the captain said. "And don't tell anyone what you have told me."

The captain turned to his soldiers. He gave them an order.

That night the big gates of the city opened. Two hundred foot soldiers, seventy men on horses, and two hundred men with spears marched through the gates. People in the streets watched. But only the soldiers knew that Paul was riding with them.

Paul got away from his enemies that time. But they would never stop trying to kill him. Paul knew that. But there was something else Paul knew. God was with him wherever he went. So Paul was not afraid.

Story based on Acts 21:26—23:31.

❦

Something to Think About: Why did the Roman captain have Paul taken to another city? Who was really protecting Paul? Will He protect you?

*Illustration by
Fred Schnaple,
1936*

160

Shipwrecked

The Lord spoke to Paul and said, "Take courage! As you have told others about Me in Jerusalem, you will also testify in Rome."

So Paul asked to be tried by the Roman emperor in Rome. It was a Roman citizen's right to request this, so Paul was sent to Rome. He would get to Rome as the Lord had said.

Some men stood on the dock beside a big ship. One was the captain of the ship, his helper, a Roman officer, and God's missionary, Paul.

"We must stay in this city until winter is over," Paul said. "If we go now, the ship may get caught in a storm and sink. People might be lost in the sea."

The Roman officer shook his head. "No," he said. "We will sail as soon as the wind is right."

The next day they sailed for Rome. They went out into the sea. Suddenly a storm came up. It blew the ship farther and farther into the great sea. The wind whistled. Giant waves slapped the ship back and forth. The storm raged on and on.

"We will all be drowned," the sailors cried. But they worked hard to keep the ship from sinking. At last they gave up. They were cold and tired. They were sick and afraid. All but Paul.

"Don't give up," Paul said. "Last night an angel of God spoke to me. He said no one will be lost."

The wind kept on blowing. The ship rocked back and forth. One morning the sailors cried out, "Land! Land!" They raised the big sail to catch the wind. They headed the ship toward shore.

All at once the ship hit a sandbar. Waves beat upon the ship. The ship rocked like a cork on a bubbling sea. It began to break into pieces.

"Save yourselves if you can," the Roman officer shouted.

Men jumped into the sea: sailors— Roman soldiers—passengers—Paul— the captain of the ship. Some swam to shore. Some held onto wood from the ship. They let the waves carry them to land.

The captain counted the men. There were 276. God's promise had come true. Every man was safe. They were on the Island of Malta.

While there, the Roman captain allowed Paul to preach to the people from the island. Many were healed and converted.

When spring came, they set off on another ship and arrived safely in Rome.

Story based on Acts 27—28:1-16.

❦

Something to Think About: How did Paul know that everyone would be safe from the storm? When God has a mission for us to do, is there anything that can prevent it if we are willing?

Illustration by Richard Hook

162

A Book of Heaven

The Roman soldier looked at John. "So, this old man is the leader of the Christians!" the soldier said. "Well, I will see that he is not their leader anymore. Arrest all the Christians you can find. And take this old man away."

So John was taken to an island in the sea. John was afraid. He was not afraid for himself, for he knew that no one could make him turn away from Jesus. But he was afraid for all the other Christians. What would happen to them?

"I wish I could do something to help them," John said. "They have never talked with Jesus as I have. They might become afraid of the Roman soldiers. They might say they don't love Jesus anymore."

John prayed. Then a wonderful thing happened. He saw Jesus! "Do not be afraid," Jesus said to John. "I am alive. I will be alive forever. Write down the things that I will show you."

John saw a door open into heaven. A voice said, "Come, I will show you things which are to come." John saw the throne of God. He heard angels sing. He saw a beautiful city. It was the city of God.

"People who will live here have their names written in a book of heaven," an angel said. "They are the men and women and boys and girls who love Jesus and try to do as He taught them to do."

Then the wonderful thing that happened to John was over. But John was happy. He had something wonderful to tell His friends. He wrote a letter to help them be true to Jesus. They were true, and their names were written in a book in heaven.

Story based on Revelation.

❦

Pray: Thank You, Jesus, that You write our names in Your book in heaven when we trust You. Thank You for preparing a special place for everyone who loves You and gives his or her life to You.

Illustration by Fred Schnaple, 1936

164

"But as for you, continue in what you have learned and have become convinced of, because you know those from whom you learned it, and how from infancy you have known the holy Scriptures, which are able to make you wise for salvation through faith in Christ Jesus."

II Timothy 3:14,15, NIV